FINDING GOD ANEW

FINDING GOD ANEW

How I Fell Away and Returned to God Despite Divorce, Betrayal, and Personal Tragedy

Barbara Kudwa

EZEKIEL PRESS
Traverse City, MI

Unless otherwise stated, scriptures are taken from the *Catholic Youth Bible*, New Revised Standard Version (NRSV), Catholic Edition, St. Mary's Press, and prayers are taken from the *Catholic Prayer Book*, First American Edition, 1986, St. Anthony Messenger Press. The symbol "*" denotes prayers that I made up or learned over the years.

This is a book based on a true story. In order to maintain their anonymity, names of specific individuals as well as places have been changed, and some identifying characteristics and details such as locations, occupations, and physical properties have also been changed.

The author tried to chronologically recreate events and conversations from her memories of them. These conversations evoke the feeling and meaning of what was said and the essence of the dialogue, but the author does not pretend to understand why others did what they did or why these events happened.

Published by Ezekiel Press
PO Box 2324, Traverse City, MI 49685-2324
www.barbfindsgodanew.com

Publisher's Cataloging-in-Publication Data
Kudwa, Barbara.

Finding God Anew : how I fell away and returned to God despite divorce, betrayal, and personal tragedy / by Barbara Kudwa. – Traverse City, MI : Ezekiel Press, 2016.

p. ; cm.

ISBN13: 978-0-9980063-0-7

1. Kudwa, Barbara. 2. Christian women—Biography. 3 Faith. 4. Trust in God—Christianity. 5. Prayers. I. Title.

BV4637.K83 2016

234.23—dc23 2016936194

Project coordination by Jenkins Group, Inc.
www.BookPublishing.com

Cover design by Yvonne Fetig Roehler
Interior design by Brooke Camfield
Author photo by Picture Perfect Photography

Printed in the United States of America

20 19 18 17 16 • 5 4 3 2 1

Dedication

To my loving parents for helping me become who I am today, filled with faith, love, strength, and courage.

I also dedicate this book to God for showing me who the true enemy is, for abundant blessings and mercy, and for teaching me that "as the Father forgave me, so must I forgive others."

Acknowledgments

For their help and encouragement, I'd like to thank Beth, my creative coach and writer, who helped me, gather my thoughts and begin writing. I also want to thank Karen Norton for helping me write and edit and Lorraine Kudwa for editing the grammar before I submitted my first manuscript. Also a heartfelt thank you to my principal writing editor Rebecca Chown, who helped tremendously to organize and creatively compose this book in order to glorify God. Also a big thank you to Mindy Buell, who provided additional writing and editing assistance, as well as Deacon Jim for his spiritual guidance, words of wisdom, and editing. More shouts of thanks to those who wrote testimonials and to all who read my manuscript and gave me helpful input. Thanks to everyone at the Jenkins Group who provided me with help in making this book possible, and finally, thank you to my family, friends, and all my prayer warriors for their ongoing support.

Contents

foreword: Deacon Jim	xi
introduction: How I Came to Write This Book	xiv
prologue: Tragedy Strikes Again	xix
chapter one: Not the Waltons	1
chapter two: A Twister, a Miracle, and Gratitude to God	11
chapter three: Puppy Love	16
chapter four: Learning the Hard Way	22
chapter five: Friends Don't Give Friends Diamonds	35
chapter six: Heartbroken	43
chapter seven: Miracles Do Happen	49
chapter eight: Right versus Relationship	55
chapter Nine: Shocking Betrayals	58
chapter ten: Counseling	69
chapter eleven: Fatal Choices	75
chapter twelve: Reviving Retreat	85
chapter thirteen: Finding Forgiveness	95
chapter fourteen: Witness	107
chapter fifteen: Girls Just Want to Have Fun	117
chapter sixteen: Never Say Never	120
chapter seventeen: Celebration of Life	126
chapter eighteen: Who Am I?	133
epilogue: Good Morning, God	139
About the Author	143

Foreword by Deacon Jim

Through her book *Finding God Anew*, Barbara Kudwa takes us on a walk through life. We begin with so much energy and optimism, especially as we get out of high school, experience first love, and are ready to take on challenges with gusto. Working as a minister for almost seventeen years, I've listened to people describe the emotional roller coaster they experience as the stuff of life happens.

This pattern of dreams and disillusionment happens to everybody. The "stuff" may be a money problem. It may be a marriage problem or an illness or an addiction. It may be a terrible accident or tragedy. We don't plan any of it, but for most of us, things happen that burst our bubble and send us into a crisis of self-worth that makes us question our faith and wonder where to go next. The saddest part is that people often feel alone when this stuff hits. As Barbara says in her book, we are "not the Waltons" anymore. When stuff happens, most of us don't have Mom and Dad, Grandma and Grandpa, and a boatload of extended family next door to remind us that hard times are not new and neither is finding a way out.

In *Finding God Anew*, Barbara gives us a companion along the road of life, sharing the intimate details of the bombshells that shattered many of her dreams and explaining how she found the road to peace. In this book, she narrates tales of romance and disappointment. She shares personal tragedies of shock and loss.

In *Finding God Anew*, we find experiences that we share with Barbara as well as other events that we thank God did not happen to us. Throughout, Barbara is forthright in chronicling the experiences that shaped, crushed, and restored her life, providing a window into her experiences and emotions. In describing a climactic event, a murder, and a suicide, she provides the feeling side of what for many individuals around her is just news.

This is a book of hope. By holding nothing back in sharing her experiences, Barbara offers a window into her feelings and emotions through a life full of challenges. These challenges include jobs and marriages, natural and man-induced tragedies, and ups and downs of faith. She opens her life in a way that offers common ground as we ponder things that we have suffered. Her experiences show a way out of isolation and a path toward realizing the bright light of hope. By sharing her story, we find we are not alone. We see that we are not the first and that we are not even unusual in facing major bumps in life. This is her story, complete with the fears, challenges, and emotions of living a human life. It is her story, but we can live it with her to help us understand the challenges in our own lives.

In this story of hope, we share Barbara's road to peace and experience the partners she found along the way. We find that her path to peace included family and friends, professional counselors, and her church, including a special movement within her Catholic Church called Christ Renews His Parish. Foremost in every step of her path is her relationship with God. The amazing thing we find walking emotionally with

Barbara is that most of the lifelines available to her are available to all of us. We just have to be open to and accept them.

While our faith reminds us that God offers unlimited power and mercy, scripture reminds us that we are expected to be good stewards of God's gifts and to use them. As God gives us the people and tools to move from lost to found, we need to constantly look for those gifts and say "Yes" when we see them. This is where hope turns the burdensome stuff of life into peace. In a diligent walk with God, saying "Yes" to the gifts He gives, we find that the last part of the cycle of dreams and disillusionment is joy.

It is there for us. Barbara Kudwa shows us how.

INTRODUCTION

How I Came to Write This Book

Use me, then, my Savior, for whatever purpose,
and in whatever way, you may require.
Here is my poor heart, an empty vessel; fill it with your grace.
Here is my sinful and troubled soul;
quicken it and refresh it with your love.
Take my heart for your abode;
my mouth to spread abroad the glory of your name;
my love and my powers, for the advancement
of your believing people;
and never suffer the steadfastness and confidence
of my faith to abate;
so at all times I may be enabled from the heart to say,
"Jesus needs me, and I am his."

—"Use Me" by Dwight L. Moody

Over the past decade, I've often felt nudged to write a book. Just as quickly, I've found myself asking why followed by countless reasons why not. With so many larger tragedy stories to tell, why is my story worth sharing?

One day, while praying in silence, a light clicked on. There was a reason I'd experienced a series of tragedies, miracles, and healings. I was to glorify God and write about how He had impacted my life and answered my prayers. I was also to write about my many prayers that I thought went unanswered. My life experiences have taught me that prayers are answered "all in God's plan and time, not mine," but it took me years to understand that.

I did not know how to begin writing my story, and since I wasn't sure I wanted to make my decisions and tragedies public, I decided to turn my back on this notion. When it kept reappearing, I asked God how I was supposed to write a book when I lacked even the most basic writing experience.

God responded by putting a writer by my side during a life-changing religious retreat, but I continued to be disobedient and didn't ask for help. My fears were larger than my faith, but the Holy Spirit kept nudging me at all times of the day and night.

Finally, I took a piece of paper and wrote, "God answered my prayers. I was never left alone through all my tragedies. There's always hope. Miracles are real. The key is to keep praying and believing. The end."

Needless to say, the nudging continued. I guess God didn't appreciate my lack of detail, so I finally sat down and began to write.

After six months, I concluded the task was impossible. There was too much to say, and it was all too difficult and personal to write about. I gave up, but God did not. The next thing I knew, at a wedding reception,

God placed a writing coach in my life. I decided to give the book one last try, and my coach and I worked together for several months.

Looking back, every time I came up with a reason to avoid writing my story, God came back with a reason to begin anew. Today, I know why. God wanted me aware of all the "God things," the things or people that He sends to help, and to show me how lives intertwine. He then wanted me to come full circle by using me as an instrument to demonstrate His grace and mercy to others.

Finally, I listened to His whispers and called my new writer friend. God directed me, and at long last, I listened. After many months of very long hours, the book finally began coming together. I sent it off to be edited and thought my part was complete. To my surprise, I found the work was just beginning when both my editor and Deacon Jim challenged me.

Another month of long hours went by, and I pondered whether or not to keep moving forward. Then God sent another angel to me. After mass at a gathering, a lady came up to me and thanked me for witnessing at her retreat, explaining how it had saved her life. I was speechless and confused, but hearing these words inspired me to move forward and complete my book.

Today, I know my calling is to help others by sharing snapshots of my life that uncover the sustaining power of prayer. After decades of falling away from and returning to God, I have found daily prayer and devotions are some of the means by which I reclaim myself.

Looking back at all I have endured and at the lives of others I hold dear, I know that pain and struggle are universal. Not everyone chooses to share their stories, but everyone has a story to tell. I think some of us feel broken, and our stories hold us hostage until we learn to deal with our issues and forgive others and ourselves.

Over the years, as I have witnessed the power of prayer, my faith has deepened. I've never fully understood why some prayers are answered and others are not, but I have come to realize that everything occurs according to God's timetable, not mine.

Thankfully, I have experienced God's miracles firsthand. First and foremost, I am saved. Through faith and daily meditation, God gives me hope. God is always there for me, in my spiritual warfare, in my sorrows, and in my happiness. Unconditional love is woven throughout my life, but mostly I am blessed to experience the highest kind of love from God, agape love. I could not survive without God in my life.

This book is both a personal journey and a tribute to my parents. In the last several decades, I have experienced a great deal of trauma, and some of it has emanated from the fact that I haven't always placed God front and center in my life. Consequently, in this book of faith, I convey the devastating events in my life and chronicle how I repeatedly turned away from God but ultimately returned.

In this story, I share how I moved to a new and closer relationship with God through miracles, priests, Christian radio, and a life-changing religious retreat called Christ Renews His Parish (CRHP), which focuses on personal and parish spiritual renewal.

My goal is to help others heal from their brokenness. For that reason, after my costs and expenses, a portion of the proceeds from the sale of this book will be directed to help missions such as CRHP, Christian radio stations, and non-profit organizations helping grieving families.

Each chapter in *Finding God Anew* begins and ends with a prayer that means a lot to me. Most are from the *Catholic Prayer Book*, but some are prayers I learned over the years or made up.

That doesn't mean I was praying these prayers at the time the events in each chapter unfold. Rather, they are prayers I wish I'd prayed or prayers I pray now to celebrate my life- and soul-sustaining relationship with God. The prayer that follows conveys my life experiences.

O God my Father, my tragedies have left me broken and humble before you.
I cry out, "Why God, why?"
God replies, "Be not weak in faith for I am the Lord your God.
I will use your story
to strengthen & feed my flock." I continue to ask,
"But God, I cannot see where to go."
God replies, "Be not weak in faith, for I am the Lord your God. I will
remove your blinders and show you the way." I profess,
"But God, I am weak of heart."
God replies, "Be not weak in faith, for I am the Lord your God. The Holy
Spirit shall descend upon you, and your heart will overflow
with my passion and desire."
I am thankful and ask, "How may I repay you, God?"
God replies, "Take up this journey. I will give you the strength, courage,
and knowledge to overcome." I am confused and ask, "What journey?"
God replies, "Walk amongst my people, share your story,
and a shepherd you shall be."

—BY DOUG KUDWA

PROLOGUE

Tragedy Strikes Again

Dear God, I am so weary of astounding heartbreaks.
I am told you won't give me more than I can handle
and are strengthening me for your divine plan.
Help me to accept that my life isn't falling apart,
that it's falling into place.
I offer you all my pain and suffering for those most
in need of your mercy.
Please put your hand tightly around mine and
guide me as we walk together. Amen.

*

"God, I'm not ready for this!"

My heart broken, my spirits crushed, I ached to hold my parents in my arms and say, "I love you."

I ached to hear their comforting reply—"I love you more"—just like God's unconditional love.

My Catholic upbringing and various life experiences taught me much, but nothing could have prepared me for shocking betrayals, shattered marriages, and the stunning death of my brother preceding two other horrific deaths in the form of a murder and suicide. Nothing could have prepared me for the community-wide and personal trauma these events would create, or the final overwhelming loss of my loving parents within six weeks of each other four years later.

The betrayals, murder, and suicide brought about nightmares, anger, and a degree of stress that exceeded my ability to cope or integrate my emotions. I felt helpless, vulnerable, and exhausted. Losing my parents reignited my overwhelming grief. Insomnia, which I had previously conquered, reentered my life.

One summer evening after losing my parents, what was left of my tanned athletic body sat slumped at the end of my parents' wooden dock. Though a gentle breeze lifted my hair, my black cargo shorts and matching shirt reflected my mood. In a trance, I gazed at the lemon-colored ball of fire as it began to drop through the clouds and engulf the horizon with hues of red and pink. Soon, the rays of the setting sun glistened like diamonds on the tiny ripples of water heading toward me. The exquisite beauty all around me was a perfect reminder of God and of my parents' unconditional love and tenderness.

Though watching sunrises and sunsets was a family pastime that usually calmed my soul, on this night, peace was nowhere to be found. I tried to cling to my faith and prayers, along with a life-changing retreat I'd attended that had returned hope to my life, yet once again I felt numb, disoriented, and in shock.

I still couldn't believe my parents were no longer here to guide and advise me. From them, I had learned to make a difference, love unconditionally, laugh often, and most importantly, to live knowing and experiencing God. My time on Earth was so very short compared to eternity with God. For at least the millionth time, I asked myself what my purpose was. Would I ever uncover it?

My mind was foggy, filled with questions and mired in emotions. I contemplated the spiritual road that my parents, who always led by example, had helped me travel. Could I survive without them? Would God sustain me again?

The answer, of course, was yes. I just didn't know it yet.

Lord, make me an instrument of thy peace.
Where there is hatred, let me sow love. Where there is injury, pardon;
where there is doubt, faith; where there is despair, hope;
where there is darkness, light; where there is sadness, joy.
O divine Master, grant that I may not so much seek
to be consoled as to console.
To be understood as to understand; to be loved as to love.
For it is in giving that we receive;
it is in pardoning that we are pardoned;
and it is in dying that we are born to eternal life.

—PRAYER OF ST. FRANCIS

CHAPTER ONE

Not the Waltons

Good morning, God. Every day is for you, dear God.
God so meek and mild, make me a good and obedient child.
God bless my Grandma and Grandpa, Mom and Dad,
Mary, Martha, Miriam, Joseph, John, Barbara, James, Daniel,
and all my nieces and nephews, aunts, uncles, and cousins.
Help guide us through this day. Amen.

*

With remnants of the sandman in the corners of my eyes, my lids slowly opened to see the springs of the bunk bed above me holding my older sister Miriam.

I was seven years old. Full of energy and increasingly independent but always eager to see my dad, I awakened at five a.m. every morning to the sound of him flushing the toilet down the hall, determined to see him off before he left for his two jobs.

After quietly saying my morning prayer, I pulled off the covers and slowly rolled out of the bottom bunk so I wouldn't smack my head on the metal bars. I tiptoed across the room, making sure not to run into the other bunk bed where my two other older sisters, Mary and Martha, soundly slept.

In the room next to mine was another set of bunk beds holding my two older brothers, Joseph and John, and my two younger brothers, James and Daniel, all of whom were fast asleep.

Each bedroom was furnished with a wooden cross that we could slide open if we wanted to use the tiny container of holy water within. The crucifix hung above a single brown wooden dresser with four drawers, one per child. Each bedroom also contained a single closet and an older desk we all fought over. I was the sixth of eight children and the youngest of the four girls, so I discovered how the pecking order worked early on. This was frustrating and never seemed quite fair.

In the dark, I made my way through the den, brushing my hand along the upright spinet piano. I was told playing the piano was one of God's gifts to me. I took lessons for almost ten years.

In the early years of lessons, the hardest part was coping with my piano teacher, a perfectionist who gently tapped my fingers with a ruler when I hit a wrong note. I started learning to play even before I could read words or before my feet could touch the foot pedals. I loved to play, but I found practicing my scales extremely boring.

From the den, I quietly walked down a narrow hallway. On one side, the door to my parents' room was closed. On the other side was the only bathroom in the house. The bathroom door was open with a nightlight shining within.

I curled up on the floor, holding my hands over the heat register, waiting for Dad to return dressed in his school bus driving clothes. Dad always told us, "Driving the bus is my recreational job."

His cheerfulness helped me imagine how much fun he must have every day.

In reality, he was working two jobs and long hours to feed and clothe his family of ten. It was impossible not to feel his love and desire to take care of his family.

My father, a big-boned man, was over six feet tall. He could appear intimidating, but he was like a teddy bear to me. He had a kind and generous heart, but none of us kids ever wanted to test him. Though I was sometimes sent to my room, I don't ever recall getting a spanking.

Dad entered the bathroom with a huge smile, his brilliant blue eyes twinkling down at me as his hands reached for mine. I quickly leaped into his arms to give him a bear hug and giggled as he tickled me. After his deep soft laugh, he whispered in my ear, "I love you." I could smell his deodorant, similar to Old Spice, as I tucked my head on his shoulder. It would be late at night before he returned from work, and I was disappointed when he put me down.

Dad, born in the 1920s on a dairy farm in a small rural area, was the son of parents who sailed on a ship to America directly from Europe. At that time, milk production was a big part of the agriculture industry. Dad's family found that their humid new climate had distinct seasonal variations and an abundance of rainfall, while the nearby tourist town was known for its beautiful lakes and sandy peninsula jutting into Lake Erie. This was wine country, and art and music were also local mainstays. My dad grew up with six siblings in a Lutheran home, and his father worked for others in addition to starting his own farm. Dad attended a public school and was very athletic; he was even named captain of his high school state championship basketball team.

Despite a promising athletic opportunity in college, after graduating from high school, Dad enlisted and served in the U.S. Navy during World War II. While overseas, he met a Catholic priest who gave him a Sacred Heart of Jesus medal that comforted him during the war.

Dad kept it in his wallet at all times throughout his life; it was one of his most prized possessions. I thought this was a wonderful testament to the impact priests can have on our lives.

When Dad returned to the states, he helped his father by working on their dairy farm. A sports recruiter who had scouted him in high school paid a visit to see if he was now interested in playing college ball, but Dad turned him down again. He had other plans. I loved seeing his eyes brighten and his face smile as he thought about his lifelong love story.

He was dating my mother, a beautiful petite brunette with an unforgettable smile who lived in the next county. She was filled with spunk and vinegar. Mom grew up with seven siblings in a Catholic home and attended Catholic school. As a child, she wanted to become a nun, and after high school, she waited tables on roller skates at an ice cream parlor. This was where Dad met her. He tried to be funny, and Mom threw a glass of water on him. Nonetheless, they soon started dating and were married about a year later, when she was nineteen and he was twenty-three. Dad loved my mom so much that he converted to Catholicism before their marriage. They were devoted to one another for the next sixty-eight years.

Dad's parents did not approve of his decision to convert, but they continued to love him unconditionally, a philosophy he and Mom extended to my siblings and me. My parents were endlessly devoted to one another, their children, grandchildren, family, and friends. Once, they even invited an out-of-town couple to stay overnight in our home after the couple accidentally smashed into our vehicle. My parents lived humbly and without fanfare, offering many quiet acts of kindness and generous giving.

Given their love for each other and their Catholic faith, it's not surprising they had eight children. When people saw all the kids spilling out of the station wagon for Sunday Mass, they would laugh and say, "Your parents are surely good Catholics, having all you children."

I always thought they had all us kids to help with the chores, and it wasn't until I was older that I understood the correlation between their faith and their large family.

My dad's first job was a partnership with his sibling as a food distributor. They kept their area supplied with snacks for almost two decades. My siblings and I thought this was cool, since we always had a supply of snacks to take to school. Growing up, we didn't have much money, but we never thought of ourselves as poor because we always had something to share.

This all changed in 1968, arguably one of our nation's most historic years. Astronauts circled the moon for the first time. Riots and demonstrations erupted as the Vietnam War and the Civil Rights movement intensified. Martin Luther King Jr. and Robert F. Kennedy were assassinated. None of those events touched us as we went about our daily routines in our small, peaceful, pleasant community. Instead, it was Dad who rocked our world in 1968.

One night, he gathered us together and said, "We're starting a new venture—picking up garbage. You'll all need to pitch in and help out."

I was now nine years old, and I blurted out, "That's gross!"

Dad laughed and said, "There's one thing this world will never run out of, and that's garbage."

We all chuckled, but after a few minutes, John asked, "What will we bring for a school snack? We can't take garbage."

Our parents laughed even harder and told us not to worry.

The next Sunday, all eight of us followed Dad and Mom up to the altar after Mass to receive a special blessing on our new venture. Dad had experienced a vision, and with courage and faith in God, he and Mom ventured into their own waste management company.

Our family lived in the country about ten miles west of town. We owned a used truck that Dad fitted with sheets of wood to enclose the truck bed. This became his first garbage truck. On one side of the truck was the company's name. Later, reflecting Mom and Dad's sense of humor, they proudly added the word "Garbologist" to indicate "a degree in which one studies garbage."

Thanks to their faith, trust, ethics, and hard work, the business became extremely successful. Dad and Mom showed us how to always obey God, and in turn, God provided for our family.

I'm not sure why I ignored this lesson until much later in life. What pride I must have had to think I could do a better job controlling my life than God could!

Our family's large burgundy leather Bible always sat in the living room. Our parents' faith and devotion to God was reflected in daily prayers before all meals and at bedtime, attendance at weekly Mass, and their emphasis on helping others. They showed us that being Catholic meant community, helping others, learning about the Bible, following years of traditions, and singing the psalms and songs at Mass to help us praise, pray, and proclaim God.

My siblings and I received a Catholic education at the same Catholic school my mom had attended. The cost of tuition—five hundred dollars per child—required sacrifices. Thankfully, the school blessed the larger families by making tuition free for the fourth child on.

As a child, I thought the church was beautiful and peaceful. The crucifix, the Stations of the Cross, and the gorgeous stained glass windows always captivated me. Over time, I began to understand the symbolism of the Mass. When I was younger, I sometimes attended Mass reluctantly, but when I was older, I felt a need to go in order to nourish my spirit.

Since I attended Catholic school, I had a daily relationship with God, but this was a private relationship, not something I talked about with friends on the playground. I memorized all my prayers at a very young age, but I could barely pronounce some of the words. I didn't question authority or ask "Why?", but I sometimes wished my relationship with God were deeper to compel me to always make the right decisions.

From the nuns and priests, I learned about the seven sacraments. These special occasions were signs of God's presence and channels of God's grace, and I couldn't wait to receive them. I was respectful in church, toward God, and to my teachers. I wanted my faith to be solid like my parents, obedient to God.

My initiation into the Catholic Church came when I received my first sacrament, the blessing of baptism, as an infant. I'm told I cried when the holy water was poured over my head. My mom said I was preparing my lungs to sing in the church choir someday, but my only memory is a picture.

In second grade, at the age of seven, I received my second and third sacraments, the Sacrament of Penance or Reconciliation along with the Blessed Sacrament of the Eucharist.

I learned that reconciliation, the sacrament of spiritual healing, was necessary when I distanced myself from God by committing sins. First, I had to be sincerely remorseful to God for my wrongdoing. Then I had to confess my sins to a priest, who would help counsel me and give me absolution with a penance of some sort.

Confessing my sins was scary. If I didn't tell the priest all my sins, I feared I would go to hell. If I did tell all my sins, I was afraid he'd tell my parents. Even though confessing felt awkward, in my heart I knew I was safe, because I knew the priest had made an oath not to violate any confessions. Besides, he never kept a ledger, and he was always welcoming and compassionate. Over the years, I wondered what it was like for priests to witness the amazing movement of God's grace and mercy.

For penance, I prayed whatever the priest asked me to pray. Truth be told, I always said my prayers quickly because I didn't want my peers to assume I had a lot of sins to pray about.

I learned the inspiring news that, through reconciliation, I received God's unconditional forgiveness. I also learned the tougher news—that I was called upon in turn to forgive others. The problem was, I couldn't truly forgive others until I truly felt and understood God's forgiveness. Unfortunately, I would later come to realize I hadn't learned this lesson very well.

At the same time I received the Sacrament of Reconciliation, I received the Blessed Sacrament of the Eucharist, or the Body and Blood of Jesus Christ. I was excited to receive Jesus through Holy Communion. In my innocence, I wondered how my stomach would feel once He was inside me, but days before receiving Jesus, my focus turned to the stunning white dress and veil I would be allowed to wear. At age seven, keen to be liked and accepted by my friends, that dress made a greater impression on me than receiving the Eucharist.

From first grade through high school, I participated in religion class. In my early years, we attended Mass daily, and all the girls wore veils over their heads as a sign of respect. On the days we forgot our head coverings, we used bobby pins to attach Kleenexes to the tops of our heads. I was good-naturedly teased about this and about many other things, too.

My very first piano teacher was a nun, and my lessons took place at the convent, where the nuns lived. She was almost ninety years old, and I was always afraid she was going to have a heart attack. My parents were forty, and I thought they were old! I didn't want to be the reason my piano teacher died, so I tried to learn my lessons well.

Looking back, it's easy to recognize my pattern of wanting to please and care for others. Later, recognizing my fear of rejection and failure led to a healthier pattern that alleviated some of my stress and anxiety.

My church, school, the priests' rectory or home, and the convent all sat on the same block. When I was a child, I thought the convent looked mysterious, and my friends and I took turns guessing what it was like inside, since the outside looked old and scary.

To my surprise, when I first entered the convent, I discovered it was a beautiful home filled with love. The old wooden floors were squeaky, the walls held a beautiful cross and religious pictures, and a beautiful older baby grand piano sat near the entry. After my lessons, I would ask if there was anything I could do to help.

Not all nuns were stern and strict. Many were great teachers and very kind. I felt sorry for nuns because kids joked about them behind their backs and called them penguins, thanks to their black and white habits. This attire looked very hot and uncomfortable, just like my school uniform.

I disliked my uniform and never understood why we girls had to wear them but not boys. I felt frumpy in my white knee-high socks and doll-collar blouse under my large and shapeless knee-length navy jumper. We wore a school uniform from grades one through twelve. Every morning, the teasing began as soon as I stepped onto the public school bus.

Meanwhile, clothes aside, I had more in common with my four brothers than my three sisters. My brothers and I played baseball, football, and basketball with neighborhood friends while my sisters made up skits, designed costumes, and put on plays for family and friends.

We did a lot of chores, the girls working inside and the boys outside our home. Mom handled the business bookkeeping while the boys helped pick up the garbage. Before garbage bags were utilized, they shoveled it in and out of the truck at the landfills. They also mowed the lawn, including several acres of flat land, then up and down two steep terraces that ended along the highway. Our small one-story yellow home, with an attached two-car garage, sat on top of the second terrace. This meant there was plenty of room for our German shepherd to play.

The only vacations we took were car trips to visit relatives or to the lake for family picnics. When I was a toddler, my parents invested in a small lakefront piece of property less than an hour away from town. They didn't build a home on it until after I was out of high school. Growing up, we had to prime the old water well to hand pump out the water, and we learned to enjoy life's simple pleasures such as campfires, roasting s'mores, and watching the sun go down. Mom always loved sunsets—she called them God's signature at the end of the day.

I did have a close relationship with my brothers and sisters, in part because our parents showed us by example that family comes first. I felt very blessed by God's choice of my family.

Lord Jesus Christ, I praise and thank you for my parents
and my brothers and sisters,
whom you have given me to cherish. Surround them with
your tender, loving care,
teach them to love and serve one another in true affection,
and to look to you in all their needs.
I place them all in your care, knowing that your love for
them is greater than my own.
Keep us close to one another in this life and conduct us at the last
to our true and heavenly home. Blessed be God forever. Amen.

CHAPTER TWO

A Twister, A Miracle, and Gratitude to God

Now I lay me down to sleep, I pray the Lord my soul to keep.
If I should die before I wake, I pray the Lord my soul to take.
God bless my mom and dad, my brothers and
sisters, grandmas and grandpas,
aunts, uncles, cousins, and everybody. Amen.

*

The clock chimed nine o'clock, telling me it was time for bed. It was springtime, and I was ten years old. I couldn't wait for tomorrow to taste my mom's carrot cake, baked in celebration of my dad's forty-fifth birthday. Growing up, I loved to help blow out the candles.

Most of my siblings and I were fast asleep by the time the eleven o'clock news came on. We had inherited a television that brought in two major networks and allowed us to watch a few of our shows in color. It was so exciting to see the NBC peacock unfold his colorful tail feathers, indicating that the next program would be broadcast "in living color."

The clock struck eleven, and the news began. The windows and front screen door were open to let in fresh air, but tonight, papers started gusting around the living room and a whistling noise entered the house. Martha began closing windows while Miriam fought with the front screen door, trying to pull it shut. Mom headed to the south side of the house to close the windows in our bedrooms.

Dad was sitting in his chair in the living room when he heard the weather forecaster say the National Weather Service was issuing a severe weather warning, with high winds and heavy rainstorms in our area. Then he heard, "A tornado has been spotted. If you are in the affected area, you should seek safe shelter immediately. This is not a test. This is an alert. Take shelter immediately until further notice . . ."

The classic "BEEP, BEEP, BEEP" noise filled the room as Dad yelled, "Run!"

At that moment, my sister Miriam saw the ceiling start to crack. She let go of the door and dashed toward the bedrooms. Mom dove on top of Martha in the hallway to protect her in case anything fell from the ceiling.

I awoke to a gigantic boom and thought something had exploded. I heard my sisters screaming and my parents yelling, "Is everyone all right?"

Confused and frightened, I ran to my mother, and we huddled together. The hallway light was working, but it was pitch dark outside and eerily silent. Not a single sound came from inside or outside our home.

Firmly, Dad said, "Everyone stay put, and I'll be right back."

I was frightened, and I wanted to jump into my dad's arms just like I did each morning before he left for work.

It seemed like an eternity before Dad slowly stepped back into the room. Dazed, he softly told us, "A tornado hit our home."

He walked over to Mom and took her in his arms. "The roof is ripped off our house," he told us. "There's a lot of debris in the downstairs entryway. If we'd run in that direction, there's a good chance we would have been hurt. Nothing that we've lost means anything," he emphasized. "We have each other."

He paused for a second, swallowing his emotions, before adding, "We have a miracle. There's one post standing near the kitchen—the one that holds the telephone. Unbelievably, it still works. I called the police, and help is on the way. We all need to say a prayer of thanksgiving to God." Through tears, Dad softly led us in the Lord's Prayer.

By the end of the prayer, we could hear sirens outside. Because of all the loose wires, my dad told us to stay put. Once we were escorted outside, we were astonished to see the destruction the tornado had wrought. The policeman told us he thought the terrace in front of our home had directed the tornado just far enough up the hill that it hadn't flattened our home.

Our neighbors had heard the sirens and come over to help. The police officers warned us that a rainstorm was coming, so the men started to carry as much furniture as they could to shelter so it wouldn't be ruined. Mom was crying with gratitude at the outpouring of help. After a while, she started laughing and said, "Well, I guess I finally get the new kitchen I always wanted."

Just as the rain began pouring down, our next-door neighbors showed us unconditional love by saying, "Your family can stay in our home as long as you need to."

They had a cottage they could move into while we lived at their main home. Our family attended the same Catholic school as their kids, and they told us we could wear any of their kids' uniforms and clothes that fit.

The next day, a picture of our home appeared on the front page of the newspaper. Going to school in my neighbor's clothes made me feel awkward, as did the pitying stares of my fellow fourth graders. Some couldn't believe a tornado had hit our home and that I was still around to talk about it.

Going to sleep at night was no longer easy. I now understood why our dog always started shaking when he heard loud noises. Someone told me that a thunderstorm happens when people up in heaven are bowling and throw strikes. To this day, I still jump at the crack of thunder, though I'm slowly learning to appreciate God's beauty in thunder and lightening.

Months passed before our home was ready to live in again. In the meantime, the ten of us had a roof over our heads, thanks to our generous neighbors. A bond formed between our families during those weeks, and in hindsight, it was easy to recognize God at work through their selfless actions. As time went by, I saw that God had kept me safe throughout my days an endless number of times.

Passing on the generosity they had been shown, my parents soon decided to host an exchange student named Abel who was about the same age as my two older brothers. He attempted to play football and fit in with his new surroundings, but after four months, he was so homesick that he asked to go back to Europe. Before he left, to show his appreciation, he presented us with a new cuckoo clock to replace the clock on our living room wall.

The actions of my neighbors and parents taught me that we are to be generous to one another and that the Lord gives us prayer as an unfailing means of salvation and holiness.

Meanwhile, the tornado taught me not to take life for granted. As I thought of the odds of a tornado hitting our home, I wondered what other strange events might be headed our way.

Dear God,
I go about my daily life and take so much for granted.
I want to thank you for good health, a loving home,
sufficient food, and warm clothing.
Thank you for my loving family and for making me.
Thank you for choosing such wonderful parents to bring me up knowing you.
Thank you for generous neighbors who follow your words:
do unto others as you would unto me.
I have so much to be thankful for. I am truly blessed.
Thank you, Dear God. Amen.

*

CHAPTER THREE

Puppy Love

Lord Jesus be our holy guest,
our morning prayer and our evening rest,
and with this daily food impart,
thy love and grace to every heart. Amen.

At age thirteen, I was about to be smitten. This was odd, because I wasn't the swooning type. By most definitions, I was a jock and a tomboy. The only thing I liked better than watching sports was playing them, but today, I was watching.

My brother James's team was playing at the city baseball field. James was twelve years old, one year younger than me, but he stood about four inches taller than I did. We were very close and teased each other often. Though we frequently competed to see who was the better athlete, he always whooped me with his strength.

I was standing along the fence, by his dugout, watching James in the catcher's box. His teammate, Wayne was pitching today.

James and Wayne were intense athletes, about the same age, and both in the seventh grade. Wayne was warming up by hurling fastballs, curve balls, and knuckle balls. Each pitch funneled into James's claw-like glove with a satisfying leather-meets-leather smack. Wayne was good, and he knew it.

Towards the end of the game, Wayne took off his cap and brushed his black hair out of his face as he walked back to the pitcher's mound. He turned to look at the bench for instructions from the coach, but when he spotted me, his brown eyes became fixed in my direction.

After the game, Wayne nodded in my direction and said, "Hey, James, how old is your sister?"

Puzzled, James asked, "Why?"

With a charismatic smile, Wayne asked, "Do you mind if we all spend some time together at your family's lake lot?"

James nodded and invited Wayne over.

That weekend, while he threw a football back and forth with James in the water, Wayne flirted with me relentlessly. I enjoyed the attention and started to show up at more baseball games to cheer them both on.

Wayne lived in a nearby city. We began talking and laughing on the phone for hours or until a neighbor came on the multi-party line and firmly asked me to hang up.

None of our conversations were deep. I didn't even know if Wayne believed in God, but I never considered this or the fact that he neither went to my school nor my church.

Near the end of the summer, we made plans to meet. I agreed to bike towards his home and arranged for a ride back later that day. Though I asked for permission to go to Wayne's home, I didn't tell my parents our plans had changed and that we were now meeting at the beach. My parents still assumed I was spending the day at his house with his mother present.

We met on one of the area's many beaches and trails, a narrow sandy beach not far from Wayne's home. I enjoyed my scenic bike ride along a two-lane road that led me through mile after mile of vineyard into a state park on an arching, sandy peninsula that dipped into Lake Erie.

As I turned my three-speed bike into the parking lot, Wayne smiled and waved. He'd come on bike, too.

He looked cute in his blue swim trunks and a t-shirt. I was wearing my blue and white polka dotted bikini under my shorts and a blue and white t-shirt.

I was hot from my long bike ride, and the breeze felt refreshing. I laid my bike against a tree, took off my backpack, and reached for a drink from my water bottle as we started walking on a narrow sandy path. The landscape against the water and skyline was stunning, but I felt nervous and my heart was pounding.

I recall Wayne yelling, "Last one in is a rotten egg!"

I raced him toward the beach, but when I saw some rocks at the bottom of the beautiful blue water, I slowed down. I felt nervous and awkward until we started to splash one another, and soon Wayne was picking me up and tossing me in the waves. We laughed and joked until we were waterlogged and then spent the remaining magical time talking on our towels in the sand.

When it was time to go, Wayne leaned in for a long, passionate kiss, and I discovered new feelings for him.

We were both athletic and competitive; so we raced our bikes all the way back to his house, where he loaded my bike into his parent's vehicle. After a hidden gentle kiss, we said good-bye. Little did I know that this would be the last time we would see each other until much later in life.

Sadly, once summer vacation came to an end, reality sank in. I attended Catholic school, while Wayne went to public school. We lived a considerable distance apart. I knew it would be impossible to see each other, given our ages, all the sports we played, the distance, and all our homework. During our next phone call, with all the sensitivity a thirteen-year-old can muster, I gently told Wayne, "I think we should break up." I couldn't see his reaction, and I didn't discover until much later in life the impact this phone call had on him.

Sadly, my prayer life became inconsistent once I entered junior high. I was old enough to pray by myself, and I was supposed to do so first thing in the morning and at the end of the day. At first, I prayed on my own out of habit, but as I became busier and more interested in earthly activities, I sometimes forgot to pray daily.

In hindsight, it's plain to see that in good times, I forgot to thank God in prayer, while in bad times, I always remembered to bring Him into my life. This was my pattern for about two decades, which was my growing up phase that I thankfully survived.

Once I entered the eighth grade, I prepared for my fourth sacrament, Confirmation. I learned that the gift of the Holy Spirit would strengthen me in my Christian life and bind me to the church as a true witness of Christ, enriching me with a special strength to spread and defend God's word, but this was easier said than done.

I wasn't mature enough to truly understand this beautiful sacrament, and I hadn't yet learned how to develop a deeper relationship with God. I knew who God was and truly believed in Him and His son Jesus, but I still wasn't sure how the Holy Spirit worked within me.

On my confirmation day, I wondered how exactly I would feel and act after receiving the gift. My teacher explained the different gifts activated by the Holy Spirit, but I was too involved with earthly events and too afraid of God using me as a vessel to do His works.

Instead of realizing how alive the Holy Spirit was inside me, my excitement came from getting to choose a saint's name. I didn't care for my old-fashioned given name, and I knew that when I had children, I would give them modern names.

I read for days about women saints but didn't find anything I connected with. Finally, I chose Saint Jocelyn. "Josse" or "Jodoc" was the name of a popular saint, and the feminine version, "Jocelyn," had been revived in the nineteenth century.

At the time, I thought it odd for a female name to be derived from a saint named for a man who gave up all his earthly possessions to become a priest. It made me wonder if women would become priests some day.

More importantly to me, Jocelyn was the name of an athlete I'd met downstate at a meet. She was a very sweet girl who also ran the fastest and jumped the highest. I wrote a paper on Saint Jocelyn, and I was thrilled when I received permission to use the name of this saint.

My secular interests were also apparent in the fact that sports were more important to me than my full attention on God and school. By the eighth grade, running was a huge part of my life. This was a sport no one else in my family had participated in early in life, and it allowed me to enjoy the nature around me while freeing my mind of the stress of homework, chores, and girlfriend drama.

As much as I loved running, I wasn't very fast at first. Cross country was even harder than summer track and field, and I finished almost last in every practice and race. I was determined to improve my speed and bolster my identity as a runner, so I practiced hard and ran on my own. Praying the rosary, while running, distracted me from feeling exhausted. Eventually, my hard work paid off, and by high school I worked my way toward the top.

Needless to say, I continued to put more time and effort into being the best athlete I could be than in deepening my relationship with God. Throughout my life, I was an average student who never studied much, though I did enjoy math and English. Besides family, sports was the biggest part of my life, so it made sense that when I grew up, I wanted to help others by coaching and being a teacher.

My dreams were simple, well within in my comfort zone, and allowed me to enjoy the summer sunshine. Not until later in life did I realize how often I put other people's needs in front of my own or how much satisfaction my heart receives by helping to make a difference in other people's lives.

Dear God, I want to have steadfast faith like my parents.
They aren't always around and it's becoming really hard
at times to do the right things.
Sometimes I give in to earthly pressures and lose my true self.
I am so very sorry from the bottom of my
heart for all the sins I have committed,
mostly because I have offended you, who shed your blood for me.
May the same blood now plead for mercy for me
before the face of God, our Father.
I humbly ask for your forgiveness in Jesus's name. Amen.

*

CHAPTER FOUR

Learning the Hard Way

Ask and it shall be given you: search, and you shall find;
knock, and it shall be opened for you.

—Matthew 7:7

Dear God, I know this will happen on the condition
that I abide in you.
This doesn't happen when I want my own will to be done.
Can you compromise with me? Amen.

*

I'm not proud of this, but throughout junior high and high school, I was what people call a "cradle Catholic." In spite of the sacraments I received growing up, I more or less just went through some of the motions while placing more emphasis on my earthly interests. I truly believed in God and wanted to live for eternity with Him, but I didn't take the time or effort to deepen our relationship, and I lied to myself by justifying some of my decisions throughout life.

When I turned fourteen, in addition to playing sports, I began working. I followed in my parent's footsteps with my work ethic and had no problem working several jobs at a time. After my household chores were done, I babysat, cleaned horse stalls, helped prepare pizzas, cleaned our neighbor's motel rooms, worked retail, and waited tables to earn money. There was no doubt that I was going to college to earn a degree and have a career.

I was obedient to my parents until my teenage years, when I wanted to test the waters without them finding out. Whenever I had time, I hung out with the popular group, and I'm not proud of everything I did. I didn't smoke because I saw people get addicted, but I did experiment with alcohol. The drinking age was eighteen, which made alcohol very accessible to minors. At the time, I thought it was cool to drink, and I wanted to fit in with the rest of the kids. Thank God we all survived and grew up to be responsible adults.

I was raised in a Godly home, but even before the ink was dry on my high school diploma, I'd turned my back on keeping God front and center in my life. It was the 1970s, and I was searching for an earthly kind of fulfillment. I didn't sit still long enough in prayer to actually listen to what God was planning for me. I felt old enough to make my own decisions and was certain I knew what was best.

It made perfect sense to marry right out of high school to my Italian Catholic sweetheart of two years. My parents married young and were happy, so why not? He won my heart, and I thought I understood love. I was just eighteen and he was just twenty, but what did age matter? He was athletic and had earned a college scholarship. Playing sports my whole life paid off for me, too, and I likewise earned a scholarship that helped offset the cost of college. We had similar backgrounds, similar interests, and were attending the same college, so we planned a summer wedding.

We were the perfect couple to live happily ever after, and on top of everything else, my parents seemed to support our decision.

Unlike my mom, I wanted to have a career outside the home. Specifically, I wanted to be a teacher and coach in addition to being a wife and mother. Without question, my career was more important to me than God. My husband was a junior in college when I entered as a freshman, and we both had to juggle studies while playing sports.

From the very start of our marriage, I found it tough to cope with our conflicting schedules and the adjustment to marriage and college life. Between classes and sports, including several workouts each day, I soon didn't know whether I was coming or going. My husband and I played different sports in opposite seasons, and both of our teams traveled. Meanwhile, we were each taking around eighteen credits and working on-campus jobs. We saw each other at the front door as one entered and the other left. Not only did I not make time for him, but I also didn't make time for God. I had plenty of time to exercise and stay physically healthy, but I allowed little time for spiritual healing.

I avoided going home because I didn't want my parents to know my marriage was in trouble or how much I was struggling. When I finally visited, my parents asked if I was attending weekly Mass. I didn't want to lie, so I rifled off all my excuses for why I wasn't attending church and prepared myself to be lectured.

Calmly, they said, "Think about all the things you are thankful for. After reflecting, ask yourself if you have one hour a week to pray and thank God. Are you going to Mass to be entertained or to give thanks? If the music isn't appealing, then concentrate on the meaning of the words. Bottom line, don't use excuses to cut down your faith. Attending Mass is about giving thanks and praise, hearing and learning about His words, and joining a community as you build your relationship with God. You need God in your life to survive."

Their final words were, "Throughout life, if you want something bad enough, you will find a way."

I was very thankful to have my parents guiding and watching over me, but without God in my life to bring my husband and me together, our marriage stayed broken. After he graduated and I completed my first two years of college, we moved back home. I intended to work on our marriage and finish school later, but our marriage ended in divorce, a matter of civil law. Because I hoped to remarry in the Church and have children someday, I began the process of filing for an annulment.

In the annulment process, the Church seeks to understand whether my marriage was valid in a sacramental sense in the first place. This process involves answering a series of questions to explain why the marriage was never valid in the Church. The process was partly healing and partly embarrassing. Facing the issues in my marriage helped me begin to heal, but it was embarrassing to ask others to address personal questions about our marriage.

Emotions and issues were unearthed that I would rather forget, such as my failure to keep God part of my life and the sadness and tears involved in writing at length about various decisions and heartaches during the marriage.

Over a year after the divorce, I was granted a Catholic annulment, but I felt like a failure. I had broken my parents' hearts, God's heart, and my own heart. I needed to find hope.

With a failed marriage behind me at age twenty, my parents showed me how important it was to have a personal relationship with God. Once I started attending weekly Mass again, I began to feel like I was on the right path. It felt healing to be home, surrounded by the love and support of my family. I needed their support and understood once again how very important family was.

Although I'd only completed two years of college, I discovered a high school head coaching position available locally. I applied, and in spite of my youth, was hired. I knew I couldn't make a living just coaching, so I answered an ad and landed a second job working flexible hours in a dentist's office.

Following in my father's footsteps, I also decided to get my commercial driving license (CDL) so that I could drive athletes on a school bus to and from sporting events.

This was not an easy feat. Parallel parking a bus between two orange cones without much room to spare was so difficult that I almost gave up. With my father's encouragement, I kept at it, and I felt victorious when I received my CDL.

I coached for several years and absolutely loved helping the athletes. They touched my heart, and I hoped to make a difference in their lives like they were in mine. I was happy, but something was missing. I was still searching for something special to complete me. God and prayer were in my life, but only on a surface level. I attended weekly Mass, but I didn't take part in any of the ministries or extra activities our parish offered. I found myself too busy with work, coaching, and planning my return to college.

Soon, I landed a job waiting tables at a popular new restaurant in town. The owner saw that I was a hard worker and appreciated that I had good grades along with being a college athlete. My waitress tips allowed me to move forward with my plan to complete my education.

Twice a week, I began driving almost two hours to college and another two hours back home again to work as a waitress and continue coaching. The drive got old really fast, and because my tips were so incredible, I sometimes thought about giving up my education.

Mom and Dad showed me by example that we all have a guardian angel and saints protecting us. Their automobile and truck both displayed a pewter Saint Christopher miraculous medal clipped to the visor. St. Christopher was the patron saint of travelers, among other things. Prayers are very powerful, and I knew they helped keep me safe and protected through my travels, so I too purchased a Saint Christopher medal and clipped it to my visor.

One day, I actually saw how prayer and my guardian angel protected me when I was driving and hit black ice. My car went into a spin and hit a snow bank before rolling into a cornfield, and I didn't receive a single scratch. On the contrary, I felt a calm come over me, and I knew everything was going to be all right.

Toward the end of summer my senior year of college, I took a day off to go water skiing with my family at our home on the lake. This was now a rare treat, and I was happy to be with them and surrounded by their love. I was tired of school, tired of commuting to and from college, and tired of working hard and fast at the busiest restaurant in town.

I was slalom skiing behind our black Mastercraft boat and had just jumped the wake to race the boat when it unexpectedly turned in my direction, creating some slack in the ski rope. The next sequence happened in a blink.

I assumed the boat would turn back in the other direction, so I started pulling the extra rope toward me. I planned to release it as soon as the boat turned. Looking down as I started dropping into the water, I noticed the rope wrapped around my right hand. As quickly as I could, I started pushing the rope off my arm with my left hand.

The boat slowed after I fell, but for a split second I was pulled under the water until the rope released from my hand.

When I popped to the surface, gasping for air, I felt a tingling sensation.

Looking down, I saw blood gushing out of my hand. I recalled the movie *Jaws*, and my scream echoed across the lake. When I pulled my hand out of the water, I saw that part of my right middle finger was missing.

With the boat heading towards me, my shock quickly evaporated. On my middle digit, I had a partially torn off fingertip with jagged bone exposed and a hanging layer of skin that I didn't want anyone to see.

I was hurried to shore, and my sister Miriam rushed me to the hospital. The doctor was able to save three-quarters of my finger, but since I was right handed, it took some time to adapt to my injury. There were adjustments, but I could still do most things like hold a pen, play the piano, and play sports, and everyday tasks became easier over time. I was self-conscious at first, but eventually I learned to make light of my injury and to take the jokes with a sense of humor. When playing charades, for example, I'd put up three fingers only to have someone ask, "Two and half words?"

I was thankful I'd only lost my finger and not my whole hand or arm, but my ongoing guilt at being divorced made me wonder if the accident was a consequence of that decision. It took many years before I realized that God doesn't work that way and that this was a drift into superstition. Once I truly understood that God's mercy was relentless, my guilt disappeared. I needed to allow God's will be done, not mine. At this point in my life, I still had a lot to learn about the nature of God.

At the age of twenty-five, I was very proud of myself for completing four years of college. Over the years, my career plans had changed from being a teacher and coach to an executive secretary to going into business and finally into law. When I finally graduated, I was more than ready to start my new life and a real career. To my surprise, much later in life I learned that I needed a couple of classes to complete my major in business.

I returned home for the summer to look for a job but was disappointed to discover that in spite of my college degree, starting salaries were just above minimum wage. My two oldest sisters lived south of Boston, so it made sense to look there for a job.

I lacked the confidence and finances to even think about law school, so I applied for a paralegal position at a large law firm. I was excited to be offered a job that would commence around Labor Day. In the meantime, to keep active, I worked, ran and played co-ed softball.

During the middle of the summer, just when I least expected it, my heart began to beat faster. I had detected someone laughing and smiling at me across the room, a tall and handsome man with brilliant bright eyes who reminded me of my dad. We started to date and kept in daily touch, but at the end of the summer, I stuck to my plans and moved to live with my sister.

It didn't take long for my new boyfriend to follow me to Boston. After a year, we went home at Christmastime and were married. I was twenty-seven, and he was thirty-one. My first marriage was already annulled and he had never been married, so we were able to marry in the Catholic Church after preparing with a priest in Boston. I enjoyed this priest and his sermons during mass, and I'd become a member of a charismatic prayer group.

My new husband and I continued to attend mass after we married. We were in love, we were both Catholic, and we shared the same dreams. Nothing could go wrong this time, and I was all set to move forward spiritually, building a closer relationship with God.

For the first time in my life, I truly felt the presence of Jesus. For the first time, I felt nourished and spiritually close to God. I was happy and fulfilled, and I felt complete. I yearned to have God nourish my soul through communion, and I attended church every Sunday so that my soul could be inflamed with God's love. I never wanted to be separated from Him again. I also continued attending my sister's charismatic meetings whenever I could to witness miracles and observe people talking in tongues.

Though I started reading my Bible daily with the goal of completing it from start to finish, after a month or so, I became discouraged.

Instead of getting help or taking the time to go to a Bible study class, I set it aside. Soon, whole weeks passed without me picking up the Bible.

Meanwhile, I loved how my job challenged me daily. My husband worked a blue-collar job that helped pay the bills, but this wasn't his dream job. The only long-term plan we had was to live happily ever after and to someday have children.

Because my career was demanding, I began spending long hours at work. After a full day helping the attorneys at the courthouse, I'd go back to the law office to prepare for the following day. I wanted to learn as much as I could to determine if law was a viable career for me.

In hindsight, I can see that my marriage slowly but surely began taking a back seat to my career, right next to my relationship with God. Caught up in the hustle and bustle of work, I allowed earthly goals and career opportunities to take precedence over eternity goals with God. Before long, the devil engaged in battle upon our marriage, and my husband and I started down the path of disagreements, accusations, and unhappiness.

After an unexpectedly rocky first year of marriage, my husband moved back home. I didn't want to leave my job or prospective career, and I hoped he would change his mind and return, but instead he filed for divorce.

I returned home to discuss reconciling. I agreed to quit my job, walk away from my career, and move back home with my husband. I had no intention of being divorced again, and we both agreed to move forward with our marriage commitment.

In spite of our reconciliation, I felt like I was on a roller coaster. I needed to embrace my faith, God's words, and His unconditional love while holding on to Him in my thoughts, words, and actions, but this wasn't easy to do.

After moving home, I found a job as a secretary, and my husband continued his job working out of town. I accepted my new life and clung to family and friends while our relationship healed. We played sports together and went out on dates. Before long, I realized that God's plan was for me to become a mother, a job with much more importance than anything I'd ever done.

One year later, I was thrilled to learn I was pregnant. At every doctor's appointment, I was amazed to see how our baby was developing. My body was changing, and so was I. Having a child brought my husband and me closer, and soon we were blessed with a beautiful baby.

The miracle of birth was the greatest gift I'd ever received. I felt blessed that God had chosen me to be the mother, and I knew His plan was unfolding right in front of my eyes. Knowing our precious child depended on us put a different perspective on life.

I had always loved children, but I'd thought I'd have a career before starting a family. Soon, I discovered just how much I loved being a mom. I wanted to stay home with my child, but my work provided health insurance for our family, so I continued working full time.

Two years later, I was blessed to discover I was pregnant again, but around the fourth month of my pregnancy, I miscarried. This was more than just a miscarriage; I lost an infant I had dreamed of holding, loving, playing with, and nurturing. Afterwards, I felt very empty and alone. A piece of me was missing, and I didn't know how to move forward.

I recall my husband looked devastated too, but he asked to go hunting to deal with the loss. I was left upset, angry, and alone to try to process the loss of our child. I wondered why my body had rejected this precious life. I felt like a failure, and I was angry with God.

In tears, I called my mom, who calmed me by talking about her first baby, a daughter who was stillborn.

This shocked me. I hadn't known she'd lost a baby, or that she'd used that baby's name as my first two sisters' middle names. My parents are very private about personal and financial issues, so I probably shouldn't have been surprised. I was just glad my mom could talk to me and comfort me. I was thankful God had led me to call her.

My sadness eventually began to fade, and in two more years, I was excited and nervous to learn I was pregnant again, but this pregnancy too became difficult. I began bleeding, and an ultrasound revealed an anomaly.

I clung to God's plan for this baby and started praying daily for the child to be healthy. I was still working to build a more meaningful relationship with God, faithfully praying and praising Him each week at Mass, and this was a big test of my faith.

Just after my seventh month, slowly leaking fluid and bedridden, I finally reached for my Bible and began reading about courage, fear, love, hope, and God's promises.

God answered my prayers, and we were blessed with another beautiful healthy child.

I was grateful whenever my husband was home, as he worked out of town and was often gone for many days at a time. When he was home, he was very attentive to our children and showed them lots of love and affection. Our children were always happy and played, ate, and slept well. I was thrilled and blessed to have two healthy babies, but all too soon, I had to return to work.

Each day, I felt guilty dropping our children off at daycare and working long hours in a job I didn't love, and I became upset that their dad was gone so much. Almost immediately after returning to work, I began to feel exhausted and abandoned. How did other women whose husbands worked out of town manage to work full time, care for their children, and maintain a happy marriage?

Over the course of a year, resentment, anger, and frustration built. I felt the devil once again engaged in warfare upon our marriage, this time causing me to entertain thoughts of divorce. I was angry and resentful that I'd given up my career and moved back home only to feel abandoned. I felt frustrated and alone, married but more or less without a husband.

We began counseling, but to no avail. Heavy on my mind was the impact a divorce would have on our children. Learning that divorce could be better for them than being raised in an environment of constant tension was reassuring. Bottom line, our differences were irreconcilable, and our marriage ended after eight years, when our children were about six and two years old. Looking back while going through my second annulment, I wonder why I didn't ask a priest sooner to help bring us together by using God as our tool for survival.

Being divorced a second time caused me deep shame. I felt that I had failed our children, God, my family, and myself, and I was afraid our children would never forgive me. The hole in my heart grew so large that I did not feel lovable or beautiful. I was thirty-five years old, twice divorced, and the single mother of two small children.

In spite of my heartbreak, guilt, and anger, I was determined to make a good life for our children, and my main goal was their happiness. I gave them the unconditional love my parents continued to show me, and I wanted them to know that as long as they had God, you had hope.

Life wasn't easy, but I tried to stay close to God. For the first time, I began listening to Christian radio music and commentary, and the music calmed me and lifted my sprits while the commentary gave me hope. I wished I'd given these channels a chance to touch my soul before now. Previously, whenever I'd chanced upon a Christian station, I'd turned the channel, my mind made up that all these stations did was ask for money. Now I felt differently, and I was grateful for the solace and joy I felt when I tuned in.

Meanwhile, I continued to thank God for my precious children, God's greatest gifts to me, whom I loved with all my heart.

Good morning, God. I need your help to surrender my mind
and thoughts to you.
I understand I have free will and have not always acted
upon your life choices for me.
I pray you will help guide me, teach me, and strengthen me
to have an eternal perspective,
having only Godly actions and decisions that lead me
to you for eternity.
I pray that I will reject materialism and worldly values
and put you first in my life.
Through your mercy, your passion, and death,
I pray you can forgive all my sins
and bless me with your grace so I can live with you
happily in eternity.
I ask this through Jesus Christ my Lord, Amen.

*

CHAPTER FIVE

Friends Don't Give Friends Diamonds

Good morning, God.
I continually need your help and your grace.
Let me abide in you and you abide in me
that my prayers may be heard. Amen.

*

When they were old enough to go to school, my children began attending the same Catholic school I had graduated from. I wanted them to be taught in an atmosphere where God and prayers were allowed and freely discussed, where they could learn more about God, build a relationship with Him, and come to understand the sacraments they would receive.

As I drove them to school and daycare each morning, I always smiled as they asked me perplexed questions about God. We attended Mass together each week and prayed daily at meals, and I felt grounded. I had a daily relationship with God that further deepened my faith, and He was once again the author of my life. I was consciously living through His goodness, mercy, and love. I always tried to pray in a quiet area so I could hear what God was saying to me, and He continued to open up opportunities for me as I listened and obeyed His will rather than my own.

I was now working as a full-time financial advisor for a full-service brokerage firm. This didn't come without sacrifices. It took months of studying early in the morning or late after the kids were asleep to successfully pass my tests to be licensed, but the hardest part was leaving my children for over a month while receiving my training out west. My family supported the kids in my absence, and I called often and tried to plan out a daily routine to enhance their stability.

After I returned, in my spare time, I coached my children's several different sports teams, took them to the beach and park to play, painted and created arts and crafts with them, and traveled with them to see my parents in Florida. Our lives were busy but exciting, and I held tightly to the many fond memories we were making.

I was making decisions based on what I thought would make God happy, and both children welcomed God into their lives. What's more, they were grounded and beautiful inside and out. I loved them to the moon and back and was very proud of both of them.

I felt very blessed when I was selected to train in a women's management program for my financial securities firm. The financial world lacked women managers, and my hard work in building up my business was paying off, along with being obedient to God's will.

During this two-year program, I continuously sought clients and made phone calls to small business owners, offering to review their retirement plans. I also established a monthly newsletter and held seminars for women offering financial advice about preparing for the future.

At long last, I was able to comfortably support my children. Our lives were normal and busy, maybe even too busy, but God was at the center of my life, and I was happy with the joy He brought each day. I was determined not to falter in my daily relationship with God.

One day, I called a local business owner in the hopes of getting a new account. This was the father of my first boyfriend way back when I was thirteen years old, or so I thought. When the receptionist put me through to the owner, I heard a man say, "Hello."

I replied with a friendly, "Hello, Mr. Woods. This is Barbara. I'm a local financial advisor. Would you be willing to let me look over your company's retirement plan to determine how well it's working for your employees?"

He agreed, and we made plans to meet at a nearby restaurant later that week.

As I approached the table with my laptop, I gasped. The man sitting there with a full beard wasn't Wayne's father; it was Wayne. I hadn't seen him in years, and I couldn't understand why he didn't look surprised.

Confused, I said, "I'm here to meet your dad. Maybe we can catch up another time."

He explained that his father was away for the winter and that I'd made the appointment with him, so I sat down.

Our meeting lasted several hours. We talked business, but we mostly talked about ourselves. I learned that Wayne was divorced and had one child about five years old who lived northeast with her mother an hour away. I told him about my divorces and my two children who were now almost three and seven years old.

At the end of the meeting, Wayne walked me to my car and leaned over for a kiss. Caught off guard, I drove away wondering if our meeting was fate or if God somehow had a hand in it. Later in life, I would discover that Wayne's memory of the phone call and meeting was a little different than mine.

Wayne's charisma made him charming and interesting to me. He was spontaneous and made me laugh. In the weeks that followed our lunch meeting, I received phone calls, cards, flowers, and notes on my windshield. I could see Wayne enjoyed being romantic and thoughtful as he brought me dinners at work.

Several months later, on my birthday, Wayne stopped by my home after my children had gone to bed with chocolate-covered strawberries and a movie. We both had to work early the next morning, so after the movie, I asked him to leave.

I recall him putting his arm around me and saying, "Wait, I haven't given you your birthday gift yet. Can we sit back down on your couch before I leave?"

I replied, "You didn't have to get me anything."

Grinning, Wayne handed me a small box.

"I can't accept this gift," I snapped.

He chuckled. "It's not what you think."

I nervously opened the small box to reveal an expensive local jeweler's name.

He beamed and begged, "Open it up."

Skeptical, I opened the gift to reveal sparkling diamond earrings. I was taken aback.

Wayne begged me to put them on and assured me they were a gift from one friend to another.

"Friends don't give friends diamonds," I blurted.

"Well, this friend does," he said.

He put his arms around me and kissed me, first gently and then passionately.

For some time, we continued dating on a regular basis. One evening, he took me back to the same beach we'd biked to as kids the first time we were alone together. He brought a bottle of champagne, glasses, cheese and crackers, and a beach blanket. We talked for hours about life in general, the roads we'd traveled, and where we were heading. Just before sunset, Wayne popped the cork and slowly poured the champagne.

He kept his hand around the bottom of my glass, and when he handed it to me, I saw a huge diamond ring sparkling through the bubbles. He toasted our relationship and then rapidly explained how our lives would be complete if we married.

I recall the endless questions that poured from my mouth. "What happens after the thrill of the chase ends and I say yes? Can you love unconditionally? Can I believe your commitment will be until death do us part? If I quit the management program to marry you and stay in town, can I feel secure about the future for myself and my children?"

Instead of just interrogating him, I should have also been praying.

We watched a beautiful sunset, and Wayne made many promises that calmed my fears and concerns about risking marriage again. I stressed how important my Catholic faith was and explained that I could count on my own commitment.

In return, he promised his commitment to me forever, and I accepted his proposal. With that, my plans to further my career in management at a brokerage firm ended. I was going to marry Wayne and stay in town.

The next morning, I told my children the news. They were soon turning eight and four, and I wanted to see how they felt. They both liked Wayne and his child, and they seemed excited.

Many months before the wedding, we began seeing a family counselor on a weekly basis. Together, we discussed everything from which way the toilet paper should face to how we wanted to spend our retirement years. We wanted to be sure we were compatible for life. We listed our likes and dislikes and talked about each one in detail. We set rules for engaging in quarrels when problems arose, and we talked about how we would never disrespect each other.

Looking back, I can see I entered marriage as though it were a contract rather than a covenant. Our terms of engagement included rules for quarreling instead of the promise that "nothing can happen that will make me quit this."

I thought we were madly in love with each other. Our kids got along great, we had a past together, neither of us wanted to be divorced again, and we had talked through our fears of marriage, so I moved forward with our wedding plans.

Wayne wasn't Catholic; this was why we saw a family counselor instead of a priest. He attended Christmas and Easter mass with us, but he made no promise to ever attend regularly. I honestly thought praying for him, allowing him to see how God works, and being around my family would eventually bring him to mass more often. In the meantime, I was happy with our relationship, and I had faith that he would keep his promises.

After almost a year, we felt ready to marry. We promised to continue with yearly family counseling check-ups and to live happily ever after, but in hindsight, it's clear that I was disobedient to God by not insisting on premarital counseling with a priest.

In addition, against my better judgment, I agreed to a private wedding overseas on a beach and a honeymoon cruise around several romantic islands. Wayne did not want a big church wedding, pleading that since we'd both been previously married, simple was the way to go. We announced our plans to our children, and they stayed home with family.

About one week before leaving for our wedding, Wayne caught me off guard by asking for a prenuptial agreement.

I was shocked, angry, and confused. I also felt pressured to make a decision quickly. Why were we even discussing this?

Uncertainty, anxiety, and the possibility of danger entered my mind. Was he asking for a prenuptial because he planned to divorce me someday? What if he divorced me after I gave up my career in management?

Wayne assured me that he had no plans of ever getting a divorce. After a long discussion in the attorney's office, I believed all of Wayne's reasoning and promises. I trusted him, so without any family by our side, we married.

On Thanksgiving afternoon on our honeymoon, Wayne asked me to join him and another random couple to be pulled on a banana boat. I didn't want to ruin their fun, so I set my book down and joined them. As we raced across the water, Wayne tried to be funny and tipped us. I recall others landing on top of me.

After I popped up, I soon screamed, "I have no feeling from my neck down!"

The dingy boat quickly pulled alongside of me, and two men jumped in and gently slid a floating board underneath me. Then they pulled me out of the water into the boat and took me to a small hospital where I was placed upon a metal table. The doctor and nurses didn't speak very good English, and I was scared to death.

My hope was in God, and I prayed like I'd never prayed before. In my panic, I made several promises to God if only He would heal me. I blamed the accident on the fact that we didn't have His blessing on our marriage. Even though I knew God didn't work this way, my heart still wanted Wayne to marry me in the Catholic Church. I also promised to be more diligent with my prayer life so that I would hear God's will and not act upon my own.

Wayne looked scared as he watched me being placed on the table. He apologized and later promised to discuss getting married in the Catholic Church. After several hours, I was only wearing a neck brace and had regained feeling throughout my body. The ship's crew was very attentive upon our return and made sure we had everything we wanted for Thanksgiving dinner.

We had a lot to be thankful for and a great deal to discuss.

After this significant incident, not only did Wayne occasionally begin attending Mass with us as a family, but he also started the paperwork to annul his first marriage. I knew what a big commitment this was because my first two marriages had already been annulled.

About a year and a half after my accident, his annulment cleared. We completed spiritual and pastoral counseling with a priest and celebrated a convalidation ceremony in the Catholic Church with only immediate family present. We weren't merely renewing our vows; this new act of consent by both of us was witnessed and blessed by God and the Church.

This time, both sets of our parents, most of our siblings, and our three children were present, with my nephew playing the piano. Our children seemed excited and looked adorable. The altar was surrounded with Easter lilies and looked beautiful. Wayne wore dark pants and a violet-colored shirt and tie, while I wore a violet mid-calf-length casual dress.

Finally, I thought I had listened correctly to God's will. God had never given up on me, and I wanted to keep Him front and center. I was excited for our family to begin our new life together, forever, with God by our sides.

Jesus, in you alone I want to place all my hope. Take away all my fears.
You are my salvation and my strength, the source of everything good.
I don't see the road that lies ahead of me and
can't know for certain where it will end.
The fact that I think I am following your will doesn't mean
that I am actually doing so.
Please help guide me down the right path. I trust in you always. Amen.

*

CHAPTER SIX

Heartbroken

O Lord, out of the depths I cry out to you, hear my voice.
Receive, Lord, in tranquility and peace,
the souls of your servants who have departed
out of this present life to be with you.
Give them the life that knows no age,
the good things that do not pass away;
through Jesus Christ our Lord. Amen.

Several years after marrying Wayne in the Catholic Church, a few weeks before Christmas, I received a phone call from my mother.

I was now the ripe old age of forty-two and still working as a financial advisor. It was the middle of the afternoon, and I was running errands and handling appointments when the phone rang.

I will remember that moment forever, like the day John F. Kennedy was assassinated or the space shuttle blew up.

In a voice filled with despair, my mom asked, "Where are you?"

"In my car. What's wrong, Mom?"

She started to cry and said, "Can you drive out to the house?"

"Of course, but you must tell me what's wrong. Are you okay?" I asked.

Sobbing, my mom said, "I can't talk while you're driving."

Still sitting at the red light, I quickly replied, "I'm not driving. Please tell me what's wrong."

My mom struggled to speak.

Puzzled, I said, "Mom, you're scaring me. Please tell me what's going on."

Finally, she said, "Your dad just found James dead. He took his own life."

I sat motionless, unable to believe my ears. My heart stopped. My little brother, dead? My insides screamed, *No! No! No!*

Finally, honking cars brought me out of my daze. I heard my mom say, "Are you still there? Are you okay? Are you in your car?"

I pulled into the nearest parking lot, tears rolling down my cheeks. I couldn't breathe. I felt like I was suffocating. All my airways felt closed off, but I needed to respond to my mom.

"Oh my God, Mom. Tell me it's not so. How did he die?"

"I'll tell you everything when you get here," she quietly replied. "Are you able to drive, or do you want someone to pick you up?"

"I can drive. I'm coming right now." I hung up and sobbed uncontrollably.

I don't recall any of the drive. All I know is that my guardian angel must have been protecting me. I drove as quickly as I could, frantic to get to my parents. It was surreal.

I arrived safely and ran into the house to find some of my siblings already surrounding Mom, their faces flushed and wet. I hugged my mom with all my might and sobbed. The heart-wrenching fact that James had taken his own life at age forty-one did not seem real, and I quickly became angry. He had so much more life to live, and I wanted to hold him and talk with him.

Over the years, I had spent significant time listening to and giving advice to my friends. How could I help them but be unable to save my own brother? Why had this happened? What could I have done to save him? Where had his hope gone? These questions and more plagued me from the moment I found out about my brother's suicide and lasted for years.

That day, we gathered as a family to say a rosary for my brother's soul, but we were lost in grief and filled with unanswered questions. I continued to pray for him and repeatedly asked God, "Why didn't you save him? How will our family ever get through this?"

My body shook, and tears flowed like a river. I hurt to the core of my being, especially with the thought that I could have helped him, or so I thought at the time.

Even in his deepest, troubled times, James conveyed that he had continued to believe in God, and I prayed that God would wrap His arms around my brother and remove his pain.

They say that losing a child is the worst possible pain a parent can endure, and many of my prayers focused on my parents' healing. I also prayed for our entire family.

Later that night, I recalled my childhood, growing up with James. We were one year apart and had made many memories together. James was gone in a blink, and I couldn't wrap my mind around the reality that he was no longer on Earth.

While grieving for James, I began experiencing a continuous cycle of denial, guilt, anger, and bargaining. Fixated on my anger, I bargained with God, trying to get Him to punish all the people who had caused James pain throughout his life. As much as I understood that God doesn't work in this manner, my anger spawned irrational thoughts.

Following James's death, I also became furious with my husband. When James died, Wayne was away on a hunting trip. Wayne and James had played baseball together. I expected him to return to comfort me and attend James's funeral, but he did not. I had to go through the most difficult time of my life without my husband by my side, and I was deeply hurt and angry.

We fought upon Wayne's return home, as his absence caused me such heartache and disappointment. Just three years after we married in the church, I no longer felt like I was his top priority. I wondered, was Wayne's love conditional? Would my love, too, become conditional as my heart hardened towards him? I could not forgive what I felt to be his lack of sympathy, respect, and love. I lacked a resolution and my anger stopped me from asking God for the help that our relationship needed to start healing. As well, I was still trying to cope with James death.

After receiving counseling about James's death, a friend explained to me that people feel despair as a result of depression or trauma that overwhelms them. Sometimes individuals in the depths of despair feel that those they love would be better off without them. Many of us occasionally feel that life is too hard or that those we love would be better off without us, but we don't take our own lives. This is because we are able to think rationally. Some people who die from suicide believe the only end to their own pain or despair is death. Depression and despair can bring about this lie, and these individuals believe the lie.

I think it's easy to just say, "It's God's will," but I have come to understand that God calls us to be stewards of the lives he gives us. Realizing we are called to steward, we are human rather than perfect. I now think there is no reason to despair about James's eternal salvation or the things I might have done to prevent his death. God in His eternal goodness is merciful; my love for James was active and real. In the end, I am only human . . . and so was James.

I know this now, but at the time, I was inconsolable. Our close-knit family prayed together, but I felt helpless as I witnessed the depth of sorrow my parents endured. Most people were sympathetic, but some made thoughtless comments that increased my sorrow. This was when I first received nudges, thoughts from God, to begin writing a book that could help people understand suicide and the pain families endure. I pushed these thoughts away, as I wasn't a writer and had no idea how or where to begin.

Through my grief and suffering, I changed, my parents changed, and our family changed. With our once treasured Christmas gathering overshadowed by the pain of James's death, something had to give if I were ever going to heal from this incredible void. I craved a new normal so that I could start to live again.

Wayne and I had talked about me shifting from my work as a financial advisor to overseeing the joint limited liability development company that held some of our real estate investments and business properties that we rented space in. Over time, I felt secure giving up my career, trusting that Wayne would never divorce me. We decided that my new role would involve me watching over some joint investments while working out of our home doing work for his company.

I was grateful, since my current long hours didn't allow me to be the mom or wife I wanted to be. I longed to spend time with my kids to make up for all the time they'd spent with sitters over the years. Our three children were now thirteen, eleven, and nine, and I was thrilled with the idea of spending more one-on-one time with them. I looked forward to the day my husband would retire, giving us more time to spend together. Working from home would give me more flexibility in all areas of my life.

Not only that, but the kids had always wanted a dog. In the past, I'd worried about leaving a dog home alone. Now, with me working from home, it was the perfect time to get a puppy. After James's death, it was all part of creating my new normal and a new normal for our family.

We wanted a Daisy Dog, a mix of Poodle, Bichon Frise, and Shih Tzu, so Wayne and I drove several hours to visit the breeder. As soon as I picked up a puppy and looked into his big brown eyes, I fell in love. The kids were ecstatic when we surprised them with this perfect little curly-haired, non-shedding bundle of joy.

Another new normal soon became important. If I were going to survive my grief over James and my anger at Wayne and truly begin to heal, I needed to resume my daily relationship with God.

Thus began my new and improved life with Him.

God grant me the serenity to accept the things I cannot change,
the courage to change the things I can,
and the wisdom to know the difference. Amen.

—The Serenity Prayer

CHAPTER SEVEN

Miracles Do Happen

O Lord, the healer of our diseases,
who knows that the sick have need of a physician;
bless all whom you have called to be
sharers in your own work of healing
with health alike of body and soul,
that they may learn their art in dependence upon you,
and exercise it always under your sanction,
and your honor and glory,
who live and reign with the Holy Spirit, ever one God,
world without end. Amen.

My mom was always the "prayer warrior" in our family. Part of her devotion was to the blessed Mother, and she prayed the Holy Rosary of the Virgin Mary daily, asking for intercession. She also made thousands of rosaries by hand for ministries overseas, served as a lector at Mass, and ministered as a Lay Eucharistic Minister to the local hospital, area nursing homes, and the homebound. She was a great role model.

To heal from James's death and my lingering anger at Wayne, I knew I needed to continue strengthening my relationship with God. Now that I had a little more time on my hands, I was ready to follow my mom's lead.

Praying the rosary, asking for our Mother's intercession, and pondering powerful words of Jesus from the Bible helped me rebuild my faith. Many mornings after James's death, I sat up in bed and grabbed my tiny booklet called "Pray the Rosary" and silently began praying.

"I believe in one God, the Father Almighty, creator of heaven and Earth . . ."

Next, I would read aloud, "Indeed God's word is living and effective, sharper than any two-edged sword" (Hebrews 4:12), followed by, "Our Father who are in heaven hallowed be thy name . . ."

Then I would recite, "From the cross Jesus said to His mother, Woman, there is your son. In turn, He said to the disciple, There is your mother" (John 19:26–27).

I would follow this by praying three times, "Hail Mary full of grace, the Lord is with thee . . ."

Next I would read aloud, "Jesus said, Believe me, if you trust and do not falter, and you say to this mountain, Be lifted up and thrown into the sea, even that will happen. You will receive all that you pray for, provided you have faith" (Matthew 21:21–22).

I would then pray, "Glory be to the Father, and to the Son, and to the Holy Spirit . . ."

I always ended with, "Oh my Jesus, forgive us our sins, save us from the fires of hell. Lead all souls to heaven and help especially those most in need of Thy mercy. Amen."

Thus prepared to begin anew, my mom led me to be her partner as a Eucharistic Minister at the hospital, but it wasn't quite as straightforward as that. I had to work through some issues first.

My mom was always mentioning how rewarding it was to do God's work, and after I began working from home, she asked me, "Wouldn't it be great to do God's work together? Would you like to be my partner or substitute as a Eucharistic Minister at the hospital?"

Though I no longer had the excuse of working outside of our home, I felt unfit and unworthy to do this ministry. The truth was, sharing this experience with my mom would be fantastic, but the long list of all my failures made it clear this wasn't possible.

She kept asking, so finally one day I told her I was unfit to do God's work.

She smiled. "The Bible tells us stories about how God doesn't go looking for the perfect human beings because they don't exist."

She found a passage in her Bible that I marked in my own: "For I am the least of the apostles, unfit to be called an apostle . . . but by the grace of God I am what I am, and His grace toward me was not in vain" (1 Corinthians 15:9–10).

That day my journey ministering to patients at the hospital and at their homes began. Once a month, my mom and I would split the hospital's list of Catholic patients. After receiving each patient's approval, we'd enter their rooms, pray with them, and distribute communion. I was able to see and hear miracles, and this brought me closer to God and to my mom.

Wanting to expand my faith, I also began attending parish classes called "Finding Your Strengths." God calls us to serve, and I needed to know what that meant for me. Throughout the course of several classes, I uncovered my talents, skills, and knowledge and thus my strengths.

Out of God's thirty-four gifts, I soon knew my top five: activator, communications, developer, empathy, and includer. God had given me these strengths, and I was excited to start using them. My obedience to God filled my heart with joy, but my faith was tested when I began experiencing physical pain.

Like some lifelong athletes, I had to stop running due to foot pain and I needed surgery. The surgery was successful, but unfortunately, I still had some tightness in my ankle.

I didn't understand why issues kept coming my way. I kept praying and trying to be patient while I struggled to participate in activities I used to take for granted. I felt my faith was being tested again, and I was determined to persevere.

Over a year went by, and I became used to walking with some tightness. Then one day I picked up my parents to drive them to a healing Mass with the intention of praying and asking God to take away some physical pains they were experiencing. The laying on of hands by the priests would serve to show that God works through His ministers.

At the Mass, when a pastor from a nearby parish laid his hands over me, I closed my eyes and prayed with all my might for my parents' healing.

To my surprise, warmth and a tingling sensation rippled through my whole body, from top to bottom. My eyes popped open, and I discovered Father smiling at me. I wasn't sure what had happened, but I knew I would have to ask him after Mass.

Later, when I stood and walked to communion, I noticed the tightness in my ankle was gone. I thought, "This can't be real. I'm sure I'll feel the tightness again soon."

After Mass, my pastor explained that the tingling sensation was the Holy Spirit's presence.

I protested, "My parents' pain should have been taken away, not mine."

Father reminded me, "It's God's will be done, not your will." He added, "The Bible tells us to go out and tell everyone of the miracles that take place."

Thankful for the priest who was instrumental with "laying on of hands" and praying over me, I began writing a thank you note but soon stopped. Faced with what I felt was a miracle, a manifestation of God's power, I began questioning how to proceed.

I'm sorry to say I felt unworthy again. I felt blessed by God with a miracle healing, but I didn't know how to begin telling other people what had happened. Besides the people who had seen me struggle, who else would understand or believe?

Once again, I found myself being disobedient to God and saying nothing at all.

Sometime later, for my fiftieth birthday, Wayne took me on a cruise vacation that ended in Port of Civitavecchia Harbor in Italy, and I was able to spend a day in Vatican City. This was my dream! Amazed and filled with joy, I walked around Saint Peter's Basilica and the Sistine Chapel. Unfortunately, there was not enough time to spend at each location or to experience anything further, so I promised myself that someday I'd return for one or two weeks to Rome and to Vatican City, a place I felt utterly drawn to.

Later on, my sister Miriam gifted me a miraculous medal of our Mother Mary that had been blessed by Pope Benedict XVI; the same pastor who healed me at the healing mass gave this to her. I felt very blessed to wear my medal and cross next to my heart.

In the meantime, our family's schedule was changing. Our children were now all teenagers, and our family was creating many happy memories together. Though life was good, the enemy had other plans for our family, and I was woefully unprepared for what was to come.

Father, I pray for the family of all mankind
that they may acknowledge you as their creator.
Be with us as a family so that we may always
have a great love for your sacred heart.
Make us gentle, courteous, and loving in our dealings with each other;
take from us all misunderstanding so that no angry or
bitter words may cross our lips,
and grant that always we treat each other as you treated those
with whom you shared your human family. Amen.

CHAPTER EIGHT

Right versus Relationship

Dear God of perfect peace, please hear my prayer as
bitterness can have no part in our lives
as revealed in Hebrews 12:15.
May those who are at peace with one another remain secure in the
compassion that unites them; may those who are dealing
with broken relationships make room for compassion in their hearts
to allow forgiveness, understanding, patience, love, and joy.
Make our complicated relationships become uncomplicated.
I seek your mercy and blessing that you may allow us all
to spend eternity together with you, God our Father. Amen.

*

Society stresses our right to choose, but I feel society hasn't balanced this with the message that our choices have consequences that either enhance our lives for eternity or do the opposite. I think that when we are faced with temptations, we must resist them with the help of God. That said, I wish I had always remembered to use God's help when making choices.

During my lifetime, I heard an explanation that resonated regarding whether it's more important to be right or more important to have a relationship when you see a situation differently than how someone else sees it.

I gathered from this explanation that there's no right or wrong when someone expresses their own feelings and view. Assuming you want a relationship with them, your only role is to respect their statements, regardless of how you see the situation. You choose God and a relationship or you choose to show you are right and end up without any relationship at all. I pondered how courageous it is to take the first step to mend a relationship and how joyous that makes God!

I then pondered who the real enemy is during troubled times. Since we all have free will, does evil wait for us to make wrong choices and then rejoice as relationships are torn apart? If God lives within each of us, why is it so hard to love everyone? Why remember things we shouldn't hold on to and forget good things we should remember? Is it human nature to judge others by their words or actions without asking about their intent but to judge our own words and actions purely on intent?

Wishing ... If only we lived in a perfect world where no one judged another!

Wishing ... If only relationships worked perfectly, with everyone willing to give 110% and expecting nothing in return!

Wishing ... If only God's will, His plan for me, was written on the bathroom mirror each day!

Little did I know that, over time, other people's choices would show me another side to them. Tough times were coming, tougher than I'd ever known. I was still building my relationship with God with daily prayer, meditations, and devotionals, and I was going to need God's protection after I received some shocking news.

O God, I smile at the stories I was told from
an early age about my guardian angel.
In reading the Bible, book of Tobit, I met the angel Raphael.
I have heard stories
about strangers who appear seemingly out of nowhere
to help and then disappear.
I believe there are many angels around us.
They remind me that God is with us,
protecting us and guiding us.
My prayer goes out to my guardian angel.
Angel of God, my guardian dear, to whom his love commits me here,
ever this day be at my side, to light and rule, to guard and guide. Amen.

*

CHAPTER NINE

Shocking Betrayals

Dear Father, bless all parents. Help them in all their endeavors, sustain them in their trials, give them wisdom and strength to meet their responsibilities, and may their love for each other find true joy, peace, and fulfillment. Amen.

I've always enjoyed sports of all kinds, but I mostly played golf for the friendship and laughter it brought into my life, to spend time with my mom on a golf league, and later to create business when I worked as a financial advisor.

Before I retired from my position as a financial advisor, I took Wayne with me on one of my business-related trips, and he enjoyed playing tennis in an outing with my co-workers. Always athletic and good at sports, he decided to take up the game and start taking lessons.

Later in life, I asked God, "If Wayne had never played tennis and we both had been straightforward with our feelings, would he have made such hurtful decisions?"

We eventually became members at a local club with a private eighteen-hole golf course, a lakeside swimming pool, six outdoor tennis courts (two hard and four clay courts), a fitness room, fine dining, an outdoor fire pit, and junior programs for tennis, golf, and swimming that helped improve the local schools' sports teams. I met a lot of new girlfriends and thoroughly enjoyed playing golf and tennis and spending time with them. In addition, Wayne and I became friends with the tennis professional Ted and his wife Deidra.

Wayne and Ted were a lot alike. They were athletic, about the same age, and both had a great sense of humor. Ted spent many years improving Wayne's, our kids, and my fundamental skills through many lessons.

At some point, Wayne began working for a month or two each year at our home away from home, and I could understand why. This seven-bedroom piece of paradise on a gated island on the eastern shoreline boasted one of the most picturesque beaches anywhere. It was about three miles long, with more than 175 species of birds as well as deer, dolphins in the inlet, swimming pools, top-ranked golf courses, fast-dry clay courts, hard tennis courts, and a full service marina.

Each year while Wayne worked away from home in the springtime, he asked me to get a nanny to take care of the kids, now about ten and fourteen, so that I could join him. Since he was gone during the school year and our children needed me, I always declined. Instead, we usually spent about nine days with him during spring break.

Over the years of our friendship, Ted, Deidra, Wayne, and I enjoyed spending time at each other's homes and playing tennis together. I invited Deidra to join a group of my girlfriends at our oceanfront home, and one winter, the four of us took a ski trip to the mountains where we all shared a condominium.

Bizarrely, toward the end of our ski trip, Wayne accidentally skied into me, injuring my knee. The remaining trip, I took pain pills and lay with my leg elevated on pillows while the others continued skiing.

Not wanting to ruin their vacation, I told my husband and friends not to stay by my side to keep me company.

When I returned home, a very good orthopedic surgeon confirmed that nothing was completely torn or broken, but my kneecap continued to be extremely painful. Simply walking or going up stairs was excruciating, and I walked like an elderly person. I began seeing a physical therapist a couple times a week. I was also trying a series of injections in my knee that gave me short-term relief.

Over a year after the accident, I was still struggling to walk without pain. My ability to exercise was very limited, and I'd begun gaining weight, which I'm sure didn't help with my knee pain. Wayne's comments made it clear he wasn't happy with my extra twenty-five pounds, and my self-esteem took a dive. We seemed frustrated with one another, and I talked about my frustration during our yearly family counseling session.

I still attended mass, even though I was angry with God for allowing another injury so soon after my miracle healing. One day I finally woke up and stopped blaming God and feeling sorry for myself. Instead, I rekindled my daily prayer life by offering up my pain and suffering for others. Sometime afterward, I was healing and able to start exercising again. Was this coincidental, or was it another gift from God?

Along about this time, Ted and Deidra, who had briefly moved out of state, decided to move back. Wayne helped find Ted a new job. Ted also started helping to coach my teenager's varsity sports team, while Deidra began working for Wayne's company. I was thrilled to have them back in town, and I thought nothing of Deidra working with my husband.

I was now actively able to exercise, and I gradually began losing weight, which helped my self-esteem. Life seemed good. Wayne bought me a new platinum wedding band, and I bought him a new platinum wedding band, too. Given the events that took place a few short months later, I wished he'd just sat me down to tell me the truth instead.

Before springtime, Wayne and I visited our oceanfront home, where we spent time with many of our friends and golfed daily. On our last night, we went to the home of close friends for dinner. To this day, these friends and I still talk about that evening when Wayne and I discussed our plans to start living part of each year here by the ocean.

By now, one of my children was about to graduate from college and the other from high school; Wayne's child had already graduated from high school and was married. The empty nest syndrome was looming, but I looked forward to living part-time at the ocean this coming fall. I was going to miss my kids dearly, but I felt proud of the job I'd done as a mother and was excited to start my retirement years with my husband. I also looked forward to less interference from Wayne's work.

That spring break, our family was going on a senior trip getaway with several other families. Unfortunately, Wayne was unable to come with us. Every year, he invited about a dozen men who referred work or promoted his business to stay at our oceanfront home with him. This year, the dates coincided with the week of the kids' spring break.

A bit disappointed, I left for Mexico with the kids. When I returned to the states and arrived at the airport, I checked my cell phone for messages before embarking on my multi-hour drive back home.

The first message was from Wayne, who welcomed me home and asked to call him before I returned any other phone calls.

The second message was from Ted, who just asked me to call him.

Thinking nothing of it, I called Wayne and we talked while I drove home. We talked for some time, catching up on each other's week. He acted as if nothing were wrong and asked me to call him back once I was home. We talked so long that I forgot to return Ted's call.

After I arrived home and unloaded the car, exhaustion set in. I dialed Wayne's cell as I started to unpack.

He answered and asked, "Are you safely home?"

"Yes," I replied, then added, "It sounds pretty quiet for a dozen men in the house. Is everyone already in bed?"

Wayne spoke softly. "I'm not in the house. I needed to be alone." After a pause, he continued very slowly, "Remember when we were younger and you called to break up with me? You hurt me a lot. What I'm about to tell you will hurt you a lot."

I was silent, unsure of where this was going. We'd only experienced puppy love. How could that compare to something that would really hurt me a lot?

Finally I said, "You're scaring me. What are you talking about?"

He continued slowly. "Ted pulled some information out of Deidra, so now I must tell you something." Even more softly, he continued, "I am having an affair with Deidra."

Wayne loved to play jokes, and I began to laugh. "Not a very funny April fool's joke." After another long pause, Wayne said, "It's not meant to be funny. I'm telling you the truth."

My body went limp, and I dropped the clothes I was holding and fell to the floor.

Looking back, I thank God I wasn't driving while he told me this nightmare. I tried to process the words he was speaking. I heard sounds coming out of the phone, but nothing made sense. I thought, "Who is this man on the other line?"

I hung up the phone, my emotions rapidly changing from denial to shock to anger. Wayne kept calling until I finally picked up the phone again.

Screaming at him, tears pouring down my face, I asked, "Is the affair still going on? How long have you been together?"

Wayne replied, "It's been about a year and a half."

I threw down the phone, ran to the toilet, and vomited; dry heaving until my throat felt like it was on fire. I kept my head over the toilet until my body collapsed.

I'm not sure how long I lay on the floor before I heard a voice loudly repeating, "Are you okay? Are you okay?"

I slowly grabbed the phone and hung up, but it continued to ring until I picked it up again.

"How can you do this to me and our kids?" My low scratchy voice blasted away. "You promised to love me forever. You promised never to disrespect me. Why do we have yearly check-ups to preserve our marriage? You said you always keep your word. I believed you. I never questioned your actions. I always trusted and loved you."

Finally, I screamed, "Why are you only telling me this only after Ted pulled the information out of Deidra?"

We stayed up all night. I hung up on him several times, yet I always picked the phone up again to try to get answers that made sense. I was so frustrated that at one point, I went through his dresser drawers and yanked all his clothes out to search for answers. I was so blindsided that I thought drugs must be involved. My world had been yanked out from under me, and I was no longer sure what was real. I wondered how many other people knew about the affair, but later I discovered that everyone was as surprised as Ted and I.

When the sun came up the next morning, a Sunday, I could barely stand up. I was exhausted and unable to go to Mass. I called our family counselor, who returned my call immediately. I told him Wayne was having an affair and was staying a few more weeks at our oceanfront home, and he prescribed medication for my shock and anxiety.

We had previously booked a flight for me to join Wayne after the kids' vacation. I was only going to stay a week because he told me he had a tournament the following week

Our counselor suggested we start counseling immediately. Wayne had told me he wanted to try to save our marriage, and since I already had an airline ticket, he wanted me to fly to him.

I didn't argue. I wanted to keep our kids out of the trauma until we figured things out. Flying alone would be difficult, but telling the kids this news would be even worse. They were going to be devastated. They were just little children when Wayne entered our lives. Both were graduating in a month, and I didn't want to taint their celebrations with gossip, betrayal, and lies.

The next morning, Ted called me and left a message: "Deidra quit her job. We are trying to make our marriage work. Are you both working on your marriage too? Call me back."

I didn't return his call. I had no idea who my husband was any longer, and I didn't trust or care what happened to Deidra. My concern was the ripple effects of their affair on my family.

Eating was not an option. I was physically unable to chew or swallow, and I could barely keep water down. Sleep was also impossible, and I just kept waiting for my body to shut down.

When Wayne picked me up at the airport, he opened my door, said he was sorry, and tried to give me a hug. I wanted no part of it. We drove for the next hour in total silence. A bottle of champagne with roses sat on the table when I entered the house.

I was enraged. I threw the roses at him, but the vase missed and shattered on the floor. Later that night, I wished I'd cracked the bottle of champagne over his head.

Wayne tried to explain that Deidra had quit work and that he wanted to try to work on our marriage.

My insides screamed at the sound of her name. "How could you have an affair with our family friend?" I demanded. "Who are you? What happened to the man I married who swore to love me forever?"

He continued to repeat that he was wrong, but he gave me no direct answers to help me understand. Why an affair? Why wasn't our family counselor ever told? Why didn't he respect me enough to tell me the truth? Why her? I was angry, frustrated, and unable to stop crying.

On the telephone every day for the rest of the week, our family counselor talked with us together for almost an hour and then individually for about a half hour each. At the end of the week, he explained the effects of an affair. Once an affair is started, it causes the spouse to disconnect from the marriage. This usually ends the marriage, but not always.

Our final day together said it all. I can still picture Wayne sitting with me in silence as I begged him to respect me and tell me if he truly loved me. I wanted to know, if there were no consequence to his business, would he divorce me?

After a very long pause, he finally said, "I'll answer honestly if you promise not to use my answer against me in court."

Tears instantly ran down my face because I knew what his answer was going to be. I was thoroughly exhausted and couldn't handle any more lies, so I nodded.

Wayne could not look at me. Finally he said, "I love you, but only as a friend. I love Deidra and want to be with her."

While I sat in shock, Wayne continued, "I have the prenuptial papers and wanted to try to use them. I was waiting until after the kids' graduations to start talking about divorce. I didn't want you to have the business that I worked for my whole life."

I threw my hands in the air. "What am I? Just a thing, a possession to throw away once you find someone younger?"

He was silent, and I screamed, "You're a big fat liar! Take your conditional love and go away. Once a cheater, always a cheater, and with your and Deidra's age difference, I can't wait until she cheats on you, too. I want you to feel the same pain I feel!"

I was completely enraged that my husband was infatuated with a family friend and wanted to marry her. I had given up my career for him, I had promised to love him forever, and he had promised to love me forever. Now somehow I needed to start my life over?

Angry and heartbroken, my self-esteem destroyed, filled with embarrassment at being taken in by his lies, I flew back home alone. Wayne chose to stay at our ocean home for several more weeks, fueling my lack of self-esteem.

I had to tell my kids what was going on. There was never going to be a good time to convey this shocking news, as Wayne's actions had been so well hidden. Thankfully, being strong for my children kept me going. I remembered that Jesus came to Earth to show me that love is more powerful than fear and to convey how His life and death testified to His deep trust in His Father. Wanting to truly live the words "In God we trust," I kept repeating Isaiah 12.2: "God is my salvation. I will trust and not be afraid for the Lord God is my strength and my might."

Shock, anger, and disappointment were the standard reactions I saw once the news began to spread. My anxiety was at a very high level whenever I had to go out in public.

Ted called again, asking if we could talk, and I finally agreed to meet him. We hugged, our eyes filled with tears, shaking our heads in disbelief. Trauma from the double betrayal was clearly taking its toll, and he looked as awful as I did.

Ted and I went back and forth with information we'd retrieved from our spouses, trying to make sense of it all. He spilled his guts, giving specific details I hadn't yet heard, and I couldn't believe my ears. The crushing details caused another explosion in my heart. After several hours, I couldn't take any more.

Upon arriving home, I took my anxiety medication and stretched out on my bed, sobbing uncontrollably as I tried to digest this nightmare. All of a sudden, the room started closing in. I felt like I was sinking into my bed, and I grabbed the bedpost, screaming.

Breathe, breathe, I kept telling myself.

I was having an anxiety attack. Later, a counselor would give me techniques to help me calm down and find my center when I began to feel anxious. I also learned coping skills such as drinking six to eight cups of water each day and avoiding pop and alcohol. I was also to try make myself eat something throughout the day, to exercise, and to find a new activity to incorporate into my life. If I couldn't sleep, I was to get out of bed and read for a while, then get back into bed and try to sleep again. Daily, I was also to write down things I was grateful for.

Before the news, I'd worn a size ten. By the end of the month, I'd dropped to a size four.

Totally shattered, I wondered why God had allowed this to happen. I also wondered why I had let my busy life take precedence over Him. I needed some kind of hope. Through my prayers, asking for answers, I once again felt nudged by the Holy Spirit to write my story.

This seemed outrageous, as I could barely function on my own from day to day, so I threw away these thoughts and did not listen to, much less obey, God.

I did start to keep a journal, and over time this became therapeutic. Trying to figure out what was real, I began to list my questions, the times I felt confused or manipulated by Wayne, and the lies I'd been told. Going crazy at the thought of Wayne and Deirdre together, I wrote several unfinished letters that I never sent, blasting out injustices and describing all the pain I felt.

I had hit bottom once again. Once again, I began thirsting for God's unconditional love and promises. Once again, I began bringing daily prayer back into my life. But this time, as I began to read His words, they spoke differently to me. For the first time, instead of thinking that I understood, I realized that I still had much to learn.

Only later did I grasp that while I was broken, God built me back up into a much stronger and more faithful disciple.

Dear God, Let me not pray to be sheltered from dangers,
but to be fearless in facing them.
Let me not beg for the stilling of my pain,
but for the heart to conquer it.
Let me not crave in anxious fear to be saved,
but hope for the patience to win my freedom.
Grant me that I may not be a coward,
feeling your mercy in my success alone,
but let me find the grasp of your hand in my failure.
Thank you for my inner strength, Father. Amen.

CHAPTER TEN

Counseling

Dear God, my sense of being is shattered along with my heart. I want to thank you for sending my girlfriends and their referral of my counselor, Anne, who focuses in infidelity. I am truly sorry there is that many affairs to keep her busy. Please guide Anne, as her job isn't going to be easy. As you know, I am also trying to cope with the empty nest syndrome. I'm drowning. Please, I need your help quickly. Amen.

*

I filed for divorce once I returned to our family home, after Wayne expressed his desire to be with Deidra. I needed God more than ever to help give me hope.

The next months were a blur. I couldn't sleep, and I took a leave of absence from ministering as an extraordinary minister of Holy Communion to the sick at the hospital.

Somehow I thought I would wake up one morning and find this was all a nightmare. I wondered why Wayne would act so selfishly and put all our children through such trauma and allow my kids to graduate under these circumstances?

Everyone I talked to expressed disbelief, as Wayne and Deidra had hidden their affair very well. God, family, friends, counseling, and Christian radio were how I survived the shock, my children's graduations, and other people's curiosity and gossip.

Kettle bells was the new activity that entered my life to help me with strengthening and my cardiovascular fitness, but mostly it helped me get out of my house and make great new friends. The instructor was terrific, and I found a safe place to work out, laugh, and cry.

Meanwhile, I couldn't have been prouder of my kids. One was graduating from college and moving out of state for a new job, while the other would soon be heading off to college. I had no idea what my financial situation was, so after the high school graduation ceremony, instead of hiring a moving company, I rented a U-Haul and drove my oldest child and a new puppy straight through the night, over fifteen hours, to help move into a new apartment.

Weeks later, Wayne returned from our oceanfront home and found a place to live. We barely communicated, as there was no need to talk any longer, but God answered my prayers and sent me an angel to talk to instead.

Anne, my new counselor, was my human lifeline. I saw her weekly, and she eventually asked me to do some soul searching by jotting down affirmative qualities about myself on yellow sticky notes.

That simple-sounding task threw me for a loop. These days, I no longer thought I had any positive qualities. Ever since Wayne's bombshell, all I could think about was his betrayal and my anger, and I focused on all the things I did not have rather than what I did have.

It took me a month to list even two qualities I admired in myself. Each day, the assignment created more anxiety and frustration. The task was impossible, and I decided to reach out to my family and friends for guidance.

My girlfriends were extremely supportive, but a few couples I thought were my friends no longer kept in contact with me. This was hurtful and confusing, since I wasn't the one who'd had the affair. Other people told me gossip they'd heard that I knew to be untrue. This too was painful and confusing. How was I ever going to heal?

I wasn't convinced Anne's assignment was going to work, but what was I paying her for if I wasn't going to follow her advice?

A few weeks later, with the twenty sticky notes complete, I placed them as instructed all around my home, in my bedroom, on the bathroom mirrors, throughout the kitchen and living room, and on the piano and workout equipment.

Each time I saw one of these notes, I was supposed to read it out loud and think of an example of why that quality belonged to me.

At one of our sessions, Anne asked me to read one of the notes out loud to model the technique. The note she chose stated, "I am beautiful."

After reading it, I paused and let out a cynical laugh before peppering Anne with questions, one after another.

If I were beautiful, why had Wayne found someone much younger and more slender than me? Why had he pretended to love me? Why had he made snide comments when I'd gained weight?

Anne caught my eye, and I paused in mid rant and started to fidget in my seat.

"Barb," she asked quietly, "what does beautiful mean to *you*?"

She emphasized the last word as it hung in the air between us.

"To me?"

"To you, Barb. All that matters is what you think of yourself."

Tears flowed and my body shook. Anne handed me a cup of water and some tissues.

Eventually, I replied, "My head knows what the word 'beautiful' means, but my heart doesn't feel anything."

Anne assured me that over time, my heart would feel peace again.

At our next session, I attempted to read another quality aloud, stating quickly yet softly, "I am loveable."

Tears began streaming down my face as the words fell from my mouth. The concept of romantic love was unrecognizable to me.

The walls of my heart closed in, tightening my chest and making it almost impossible to breathe. Resolutely, I stated, "If being in love cuts so deep and leaves such scars, I will never love again."

In response, Anne asked me to list the people who loved me.

"Definitely God," I said. "Also, my family loves me."

"What about all your relatives?" Anne inquired.

I nodded in agreement.

"Well," Anne said, "guesstimate how many people love you."

I smiled, noticing the pattern Anne was creating. "About fifty people. I have a very large family."

Anne replied, "Now dig deeper into your heart and think about all your girlfriends who stay by your side, all the kids you coached throughout the years, and all the patients you took communion to. When you go to bed each night, recall all these people who love and care for you. Next session," she concluded, "I want to tackle this question: do you believe you're worthy of being loved? As you are, right here and right now."

Anne let me know that she was proud of me, and I left the office feeling emotionally drained and vulnerable yet simultaneously hopeful.

That night, I got down beside my bed on my knees and recalled all the people who loved me. I did this every night. Each day, I focused on and clung to my relationship with God.

I found hope with God, and eventually, with the help of prayer, I began to occasionally feel peace fill my soul. I also began to realize I was worthy of being loved. These feelings didn't last, but I found I could get them back.

At our next session, Anne asked several questions that stumped me.

"Do we all have free will that allows us choices as to which path we choose or don't choose?"

I replied slowly, "Yes."

Anne continued, "Then would you say that people are either givers or takers, with or without a conscience?"

I leaned to the side of my chair, placing my elbow on the armchair and my hand on the side of my head. I sat for quite some time, pondering her words, before I responded, "Yes."

Anne handed me a book titled *The Sociopath Next Door*, and what I read later surprised me.

Until now, I'd thought sociopaths were violent criminals, but this book revealed that a shocking four percent of ordinary people—one out of twenty-five—possess no conscience and find ways to justify their actions.

For the first time, I began to realize that throughout my life, hurtful actions I'd endured had nothing to do with me but instead were exclusively about the other person.

I was continuing to read when I heard a knock on the door. Wayne had asked to come over and retrieve his guns for hunting season. I didn't want the guns and handed them over, but many months later, one cold winter afternoon, I had cause to wonder how many people knew that Ted too had purchased a gun.

If I'd kept in contact with Ted, if he'd shared the depth of his pain, anger, and despair with me, could I have gotten him some help?

I couldn't help but ask this question, even though the truth of the matter was that I could barely help myself.

Our Father, who art in heaven, hallowed be thy name; thy kingdom come; thy will be done on earth as it is in heaven. Give us this day our daily bread; and forgive us our trespasses, as we forgive those who trespass against us; and lead us not into temptation, but deliver us from evil. Amen.

—The Lord's Prayer

CHAPTER ELEVEN

Fatal Choices

Out of the depths I cry to you, O Lord, Lord, hear my voice!
O let your ears be attentive to the voice of my pleading.
If you, O Lord, should mark our guilt, Lord, who would survive?
But with you is found forgiveness: for this we revere you.

The drama that consumed our family did not stop with the announcement of Wayne's infidelity. Less than a year later, trauma reached far beyond us to impact our entire community. The memory of that day is forever embedded in my mind.

Early that morning, with my best friend Duke, our Daisy Dog, sitting next to me in the passenger seat, I departed from my new home that had been blessed by a priest and purchased with my kids' approval. I drove my blue SUV very carefully on the icy roads towards the place I'd once called home.

Duke always showed me unconditional love. He was truly a gift from heaven and one of the guardian angels always by my side.

He kept me company through all my tough times and lonely nights and often placed his head on my chest, assuring me with his big brown eyes that everything was going to be okay.

The house was surrounded by acres of very tall pine and oak trees. As I traversed the narrow driveway, the view quickly opened up to reveal an enormous two-story home with the basketball net still on the hoop, blowing in the wind and snow.

I glanced toward the pole barn. With both heat and air conditioning, it was a great place to host everything from graduation and Christmas parties to small card parties. Downstairs was Wayne's "man cave," once filled with every toy a guy could dream of, while the loft stored business records.

With Duke by my side, I entered the chilly front room. The house had finally sold, and I was moving out. Wayne and his child had taken their belongings months earlier, having disconnected from our family and begun new lives, but the house still held a few fond memories for me.

My eyes caught a slight movement out the kitchen window. In the back yard, a small deer was standing by her mother's side. I looked at the hill they stood on and remembered our children sliding down that same hill.

I ventured into my computer room and recalled the night before. I'd worked until the wee hours of 1:30 a.m. As I was leaving, I'd noticed lights in the pole barn. A bit shaken, I'd called a police officer friend of mine to come out and patrol the grounds.

No one had appeared to be on the premises, but my friend didn't leave until I'd locked up the house. After assuring me that someone would come by again later to patrol the property, I'd packed up and driven away.

I shook myself out of my reverie, telling myself I'd follow up with my police officer friend later. Now it was time to get down to work.

After packing up my computer room, bedroom, and half the kitchen, I heard the doorbell ring. I looked at the clock and was surprised to see that it was already four in the afternoon. Wondering who might be paying me a visit, I opened the door to see my youngest brother Daniel.

I was surprised, but in hindsight, it's clear that God sent me an angel.

Athletics were important to all my brothers as well as to me, and Daniel and I were jointly coaching tonight's basketball game. As I invited him in out of the cold, I was confused. Had I forgotten where we'd agreed to meet?

Daniel looked around the living room. "Where's the television?"

"The services for the phone, TV, and Internet are shut off, so I moved the TV to my home," I explained.

He asked, "Did anyone try to call you on your cell phone today?"

I looked around. Where was my cell phone? I'd been so busy packing that I'd lost track of it. Had I even used it today?

I went to my purse and saw the ringer on silence. I turned it on as Daniel slowly started to talk, but the first words weren't out of his mouth when the doorbell rang again.

To my surprise, it was my sister Miriam. Little did I know it, but my second angel had arrived to be by my side.

Miriam looked at my brother and asked if I knew yet.

Knew what? Why were they looking at me with such sad faces?

Together they both said, "You need to sit down."

Just then, the doorbell rang a third time. Even more confused, I opened the door to find two policemen standing on the steps. I turned around and looked at my brother and sister.

"What's going on?" I demanded.

The closest officer asked my siblings, "Is she aware of anything yet?"

I panicked, and my body began to tremble. My first thought was that something had happened to our elderly parents. That must be the reason why my siblings were with me now. I quickly shouted, "Are Mom and Dad okay?"

The other officer asked, "Where were you today?"

"I've been here all day, packing." Anxiety washed over me, and I felt annoyed with his stupid question. "Please, just tell me if my parents are all right."

Daniel and Miriam assured me that Mom and Dad were fine.

The officer asked another question, his face serious. "Did you talk to anyone today?"

Why was he asking me the same question my siblings had asked me? I'd been drinking coffee all day on an empty stomach, and my body began to feel full of acid. I replied, "I didn't speak to anyone, except just now with my brother and sister."

Then the officer asked, "When was the last time you saw or spoke with your husband?"

Now that was bizarre. I began to wonder if Wayne had sent the officers to harass me because I'd called a police officer friend last night about the pole barn. Upset, I replied, "On Friday. Wayne called to ask if he could take his child's bedroom furniture. I told him yes. He came over with a U-Haul and drove off with the furniture. I haven't seen him since." Agitated, I asked, "Why are you here at my home?"

They asked me to sit down, and I immediately said, "No. Please just get to the point because my brother and I have to leave and coach a game tonight."

The police nodded toward my siblings, so I looked at them and saw tears on their faces. Miriam and Daniel slowly walked towards me and put their arms around me.

The officer slowly said, "Ma'am, we are very sorry to tell you that today, downtown, someone shot your husband."

I heard a buzzing sound, and words didn't register. Time froze. Surely I'd heard him incorrectly.

Again he spoke slowly, but this time I heard the words more clearly. "Your husband died instantly."

My siblings put their arms tightly around me.

In disbelief, I asked, "When?"

Wayne was always trying to top his last joke. Could this be a bad joke?

"Around one o'clock." The officer continued, "We've been trying to locate you."

In shock, I asked, "Who shot him?"

In complete disbelief, I heard the words "Ted Robertsing."

"Deidra's husband? No! No way!" My body began to shake. "Did Wayne try to shoot him?" I asked.

The officers looked puzzled. "No. Ted killed your husband and then killed himself."

I ran into the bathroom, Miriam following. She began to rub my back as I knelt over the toilet, coughing and eventually throwing up.

The policemen came into the bathroom and said something. I saw their lips move, but I couldn't hear anything. Miriam shook her head, and they left.

After a while, she told me, "I said a prayer for you, that you wouldn't be alone when you received the news."

"Everyone's in shock. We didn't know if you'd gotten a call or not. I didn't want you to be alone, either," replied Daniel, hovering near the door.

God's protection kept me from hearing the devastating news from the media. God also sent two angels to be my side. I was in total shock but thankful.

I still hadn't spoken a word, and my head continued to pound as my siblings explained that no one else was hurt.

Daniel continued, "Because the shooting happened downtown, they locked down nearby schools and businesses."

"Oh my God," I suddenly panicked. "What about my kids? I pray to God the news hasn't reached them yet. Did either of you call them?"

"No," they both replied.

Just then my phone rang, and it was my oldest calling from work, out of state and alone. A friend had called with consolations.

My heart broke. I wanted to reach through the phone to grab and hold tightly to my adult child. I felt like I'd failed all over again, and I prayed to God to send angels to surround and protect both of my kids.

When I hung up, I thought about my youngest, who was playing in a college game that day. I didn't want to assume everyone had already heard the news. After talking to the coach, I called once a teammate was close by. Again, I wanted to reach through the phone and hold tightly my teenager.

My final call was to my parish, asking for a priest. I had many questions, and I needed to be consoled and reassured. I wondered if I should call Wayne's parents, sibling, and adult child, but we'd already stopped communicating, so I decided it was best not to call.

Daniel finally said, "It's after five. We should leave before any reporters come by."

Then I remembered the game. "What about coaching tonight?"

Daniel spoke up. "Don't worry about that. The kids are pretty shaken up, and both the varsity and junior varsity games have been canceled."

Not too long ago, Ted had helped coach these players. Many prayers were going to be needed for all the people associated with this tragedy.

Although I was still Wayne's wife at the time of his death, I deferred the funeral arrangements to his parents. Only then did I learn that Wayne had already made funeral arrangements and had arranged for a reverend we knew to give his eulogy.

I was stunned anew. Less than a year had passed since learning of Wayne's and Deidra's infidelity, and I felt like Dorothy from *The Wizard of Oz*. I was blessed to have Anne, my counselor, and my pastor patiently counsel and console me through this nightmare. My pastor helped me deal with my trauma while keeping God front and center.

I needed God more than ever after learning of a new will Wayne had executed excluding me from business assets but leaving me with a huge debt that could have been covered under an insurance policy he'd stopped paying the premiums on. This caused many sleepless nights and further complicated matters. I no longer needed my divorce attorney, but God sent me three angels in the form of new attorneys who each protected me on different issues. With no career, I wondered about my future, a job, and where I would end up living.

Meanwhile, gossip ran like wildfire in our small, tightknit community. I was treated with unbelievable thoughtfulness and my friends' main concern was how my family was doing, but some wanted specific details to help them understand. I too wanted to understand, but eventually I came to realize that I would never understand or have all the answers. How could anyone know the whole truth? God was the only one who knew or could know everything.

The gossip just added fuel to the fire and continued to disrupt all our lives, but I refused to let this trauma keep me from Mass on Sunday. Six days after the shootings, I walked in looking straight at the altar and went directly to the pew where my parents always sat. Lovingly, they separated so I could sit between them. One held my hand and the other put an arm around me as I cried throughout the Mass.

Wayne and Ted's deaths dredged up memories of James's death nearly eight years earlier. I thought of their parents, now dealing with the traumatic deaths of their sons, and my heart broke for them as I remembered my own parents' pain. In spite of my trauma, I prayed for God to comfort them and their families.

Attending Wayne's funeral service was surreal. The church was crowded, and I had no idea if Deidra was present, nor did I care.

I attended with my family after learning that we were to sit in a section in the back of the church and would be ushered to an exit at the end.

As bizarre as this felt, it couldn't take away the thirteen years we'd spent as a family and the love we had shared with Wayne being a husband, father, uncle, and son-in-law.

Ted's funeral was also difficult to endure. I saw family members, friends, and players Ted had coached. I also caught a glimpse of Deidra. One look at her made me begin rehashing all her betrayals and where they had led. She hadn't spoken a single word to me since shattering my world, and my angry, unforgiving heart had no room to be sympathetic to her.

Throughout this agonizing time, God helped me get through each day of court. I prayed and tightly held to the cross Miriam had given me. I didn't pursue the company and the prenuptial was never used. No amount of money in the world was worth more drama in my life.

The stress I had endured tampered with my heart to the point that I had to be hospitalized for several days after an incident that at first appeared to my friends to be a stroke. Wanting to recover and be healthy, I began avoiding any interactions that reminded me of Wayne or Deidra.

I am sorry to admit it, but I wasn't like the Amish parents I'd heard about on TV who immediately forgave the teenage boy who shot their daughter. I recalled hearing the boy's parents tell a newscaster how the girl's parents had stopped to see them the day after her death to tell them they forgave their son.

I knew I could never forgive anyone for killing my kids, but listening to the reporter quote the Bible verse the girl's parents had shared, I felt ashamed. Bitterness stood as a proud guard around my heart, but I should have known that unforgiveness was going to hold me ransom until the day I finally listened, gave up control, and handed it all over to God.

As it stood, I could not forgive Wayne or Deidra. Over the next year, leaning on God and prayer to help me endure each day, I continued to work on my self-esteem with my counselor Anne and my pastor, Father David. Eventually, I began to realize that God had blessed me with an abundance of goodness and a smile that lights up a room.

When Anne asked, "Do you feel ready to start dating?" I laughed out loud. The thought was ludicrous.

"My husband defended Tiger Woods's extramarital affairs," I told her. "Instead of placing God on a pedestal, I felt he placed Tiger on it. If I can't connect the dots that are right in front of me, how can I ever trust again?"

Anne handed me a book that talked about signs of infidelity.

I shook my head and laughed. "No need to read this now."

Anne said, "If you can't trust your judgment, educate yourself so you won't get hurt again. Believe it or not, there will come a day when you will trust and date again, but first you need to let go of your past and completely forgive."

Forgive. It seemed inconceivable that I could ever forgive Wayne or Deidra for what they had done. It seemed equally inconceivable that I could find a way to forgive myself for past decisions I had made. I didn't agree with Ted's final actions, but I wasn't going to be the judge and jury for anyone. That was God's job.

Filled with pain, I forgot that we are all human and that we all make mistakes. I was still a long way from letting time, prayer, counseling, or giving up control to God bring about forgiveness and a deeper understanding. Fueled by fear of the unknown along with rage, heartbreak, and shame, I demanded answers from God to help me understand why all of this had happened.

I still had a long way to go.

Dear God, I come to you, confess my sins, and ask for your forgiveness.
I am sorry with my whole heart for all my sins,
mostly because I have offended thee.
Therefore I firmly resolve, with the help of your grace,
not to sin again.
Please help me to forgive others as you forgive my trespasses. Amen.

*

CHAPTER TWELVE

Reviving Retreat

Lord, time is your gift to me and through it, you who are eternal, enter my life and world. Guide, inspire, and help me to fill every moment of every hour, full to the brim with your presence, so that it may overflow to others around me and quench their thirst for the true meaning of life. Amen.

Nearly two years after Wayne's death, I was doing okay. Whenever new questions or issues arose, I went straight to my counselor Anne or Father David for help. I had survived about nine months of agonizing divorce issues followed by approximately nine more months of painful physical and mental issues after Wayne's death. After retaining a third attorney, a settlement was finally reached. Meanwhile, I was continuing to manage my rental property and trying to find some kind of absoluteness, my new normal.

When all was said and done, I had no health insurance or career. On the positive side, and most importantly, I had God, my health, and the blessing of my two children, family, and friends.

In addition to spending time with family and friends, I was continuing to build a stronger relationship with God, not just from books but also from being with Him in my heart through my actions, prayer, and daily intimate contact as He spoke to me.

I was looking ahead to summer and thinking about purchasing a home on the water and a speedboat to enjoy with my family. Parents of one of my kid's friends owned a local dealership, so one afternoon, I stopped in at their showroom.

My friend Cheryl was on the phone, so another salesman helped answer my questions. Later, Cheryl came outside with a beautiful smile and warm hug. Excited, she fired off questions like a Fourth of July celebration.

"How are you and your kids doing? Where are you living? Do you still belong to a local parish?"

I laughed. "Good, in town, and yes."

Before I could ask any questions in return, she quickly went back into the building, grabbed a piece of paper, and jogged back toward me. Filled with excitement, she handed it to me, saying, "Intervention from a higher being brings us together today."

Cheryl then proceeded to invite me to an upcoming local Catholic women's weekend retreat. Her hometown was on fire with the Holy Spirit due to Christ Renews His Parish (CRHP), and now it was coming to our town. With an exuberant smile on her face, she exclaimed, "It's this weekend!"

I quickly replied, "No. I am not ready to share any of my trauma."

Cheryl spoke softly and slowly. "You don't have to share anything. The retreat will be a safe place to listen, pray, and enjoy the companionship of other faith-filled women."

She placed her arm around me and assured me she would be right by my side. Hopeful, she asked, "Do you want to attend?"

Tingling sensations ran through my body. If God was nudging me to go, I didn't want to be disobedient, but still I hesitated.

Silently, I scanned the papers that talked about the CRHP retreat. These spiritual renewal weekends were designed to help individuals grow in their parish ministries and in their personal relationship with Jesus Christ with others in their surrounding faith community. Held twice a year, the retreats were separate for men and women.

Finally, I replied, "How about you give me your phone number, and I'll call you later with a definite answer."

Excited, Cheryl replied, "I'll make sure the seat is still available." She wrote down her phone number and told me to call at any time.

I drove away pondering several questions. Should I listen to the tingling sensations God was sending me? What if I didn't know anyone else from my own or the surrounding parishes? Was I ready to make new friends and trust women again?

I felt uneasy at how few details I knew. I asked God, "Am I disobeying you if I don't attend this women's retreat? Can't I just praise you at Sunday Mass?"

Once I was home, I dropped into my lounger, leaned back, and closed my eyes. It wasn't pleasant to reminisce about how my life had turned out when I hadn't listened to God, but I still wanted to try to think of a way out of this invitation.

Avoiding the call to Cheryl, I walked Duke, then cleaned up the kitchen and took a leisurely bath, one of my new activities. Later that evening, I grabbed my Bible, sat down, and began to pray. I read Psalm 136:1–26 about God's eternal love and once again felt a tingling sensation throughout my body. I realized I was being pulled to give thanks and attend the retreat.

Feeling insecure but compelled to obey, I called Cheryl and asked if the last seat were still available. After she said yes, I told her, "I want you to know that God helped me reclaim my life several times when I hit rock bottom. The least I can do in return is listen and pray. I will attend the retreat."

Cheryl was exuberant and promised to stay by my side. She ended our call with, "This retreat will be the best gift you've ever given yourself."

At 6:00 a.m. the next day, I awakened to a constellation noise from my iPhone. I said my morning prayers and thanked God for everyone in my life, read one of my daily readings, and finished with a prayer asking God to be by my side.

I dragged myself out of bed and into the shower. Toweling off, I wondered what I should wear. Cheryl had told me to dress casually. I pulled on a pair of jeans, a teal shirt, and a pair of casual shoes. I packed my bathroom belongings, fresh underwear, and a blouse along with navy sweat pants and a white t-shirt to sleep in. I headed to the kitchen, grabbed my favorite thermos, and poured coffee to the brim. Then I grabbed my sleeping bag and pillow off the chair and nervously carried all my belongings to the car.

I drove the twenty minutes to the retreat with an unsettled feeling in my stomach, but a cheerful lady waved at me as I entered the parking lot. Nervous, I drove towards her and rolled down my window. I felt better when I recognized her face.

"Good morning, Barb," she smiled. "Welcome to the retreat. How are you doing?"

"Better now," I replied with a smile. "I'm happy to see you."

She told me to drive towards the north edge of the back parking lot. As I parked, another lady appeared, welcomed me, and helped me carry my belongings toward the church.

The front doors opened into a quiet entryway. At the bottom of the stairwell, I heard loud laughter. At first glance in the room, I estimated the ages of the thirty or so women to be between twenty and eighty. I saw a few mothers whose children had attended school with my children. All my other issues aside, I wondered if God might be guiding me to the retreat to help me overcome my struggles with the ever-present empty nest syndrome.

Cheryl walked over to me with a big smile. After a hug, she said, "Relax and enjoy. We will be pampered this weekend, so feel free to let them know any of your needs."

Just then a lady appeared, asking, "May I fill your thermos with fresh coffee?"

I quickly replied, "No, thank you." I wasn't accustomed to being waited on, and I felt a little awkward.

At that moment, chimes sounded along with an announcement. "If needed, take a quick bathroom break and come right back. Please sit at the table where your name is located."

A few minutes later, as I nervously walked around the room full of tables, Cheryl smiled and called out, "Over here, Barb. You're at this table." Her friendliness made me feel comfortable.

Our table filled with six beautiful women. Other than Cheryl, I didn't know any of them. Everyone was asked to state her name, career, and parish.

When it was my turn, I said, "I'm Barbara. I'm a retired financial advisor, and I belong to St. Augustine Parish."

The next lady who introduced herself finished with, "I love to write."

Though my heart dropped into my stomach, I half smiled. Was this a coincidence, or was it God's sense of humor in action? Lately, I'd begun receiving nudges again, sometimes during the day and sometimes at night, to write a book. As always, I felt inadequate and unworthy of this request. What's more, I feared what else He might ask of me, so instead of asking for help, I ignored God's nudging.

The chimes rang again with an announcement from the director. "First, I want to thank everyone for saying 'Yes' to this retreat. As caretakers, we don't always allow time for ourselves. As expected, many of you are anxious and curious as to what the retreat entails. The agenda is on the table, and it outlines the next couple of days. Specific details are deleted. We ask you to be patient and trust in God's plan." She smiled and said, "I am happy to introduce Father Ronald. He will be available all weekend for questions and guidance. Father, will you please lead us all in prayer?"

Father Ronald spoke in a kind, gentle voice. At the end of the prayer, he sat near the back of the room. I silently thanked God that he was at the retreat. His presence made me feel much more at ease.

The director then explained, "Please, everyone, respect one another's privacy. We are bonded together as sisters in Christ, and what is spoken in these rooms stays inside these rooms. We will hear personal stories from several of our sisters in Christ. They will all testify as to how God impacts their lives. None of you will be asked to share your own stories, so please sit back and relax. Mass is going to be held tonight followed by group activities, or you may have quiet prayer time. Let's begin."

As the retreat unfolded and I sat listening to each witness, I felt inexpressible gratitude and pride. Sometimes my eyes filled with tears. I couldn't imagine the courage and strength it must take to stand in front of a group of peers to talk about personal trauma and God's presence.

At times over the next two days, I found it very difficult to absorb the pain each witness had endured. Some hurts were similar to my own, and I realized some deep scars remained within me to be healed. Were these witnesses coincidental, or had God placed them in my life at this specific time? Each woman showed tremendous strength in moving forward with God at the center of her life.

Listening, I felt a few layers of my own incredible pain peel away. In spite of how I often felt, I wasn't entirely alone, even on Earth.

The first night, we spent several hours in the church, where confession was being held along with a beautiful Mass. Confession was sometimes uncomfortable, but as always, the priest helped me talk through my problems. My enduring issue, I knew, was my lack of forgiveness towards Wayne and Deirdra.

That night Father David, the pastor from my parish, opened my heart to the possibility of forgiving. After I conveyed the depth of my anger, he asked me a series of questions that gave me a lot to ponder.

"Have you ever asked to be forgiven for something you wish you had never done? Do you think God wants you to pick and choose whom you are willing to forgive? Who is the ultimate judge of us all and is all merciful?"

Father David then reminded me, "Don't beat yourself up, as you are only human and have feelings and emotions that react to hurtful situations. Remember that God lives inside each of us. Do you remember the story of Joseph, who was betrayed by his brothers and sold into bondage yet wasn't motivated by revenge but by love and forgiveness? Continue to pray daily and ask God to enter and soften your heart."

Sitting back in my pew after my confession, I had much to ponder.

After a half hour passed, wanting to prepare myself for communion, I recalled a parish Mass and closed my eyes, thinking of the song by Mercy Me called "I Can Only Imagine."

Father asked us to consider what we would really feel and do if we saw God, and I thought about my pastor's talk on the sacrament of Holy Communion. He had asked each of us whether receiving communion was routine or whether it filled our hearts with passion. When I received God, was it a ho-hum experience, or did I respond inside with a proud and loud "Amen"?

I recalled another profound sermon about the three things necessary to everyone: "Truth of faith which brings understanding, love of Christ which brings compassion, and endurance of hope which brings perseverance."

Truth, love, and hope. I felt that many people, including myself, were looking for hope that was lost or that they were losing. Many times I'd found myself saying, "What's the use? Nothing's going to change. I don't understand. I give up. I feel alone. I have no purpose." This had occurred in my life whenever God wasn't my main focus and when I'd let circumstances draw me away from my relationship with Him.

I was thankful to God for helping me survive and for placing hope back in my life. As my mind wandered, the word "survival" reminded me of a song I'd begun singing whenever I thought of Wayne. My revised version of "I Will Survive" by Gloria Gaynor went like this:

> *(Verse 1) At first I was afraid; I was petrified. Thinking I could never live without you by my side. I've spent so many nights thinking how you did me wrong, then God made me strong and I learned how to get along.*
>
> *(Verse 2) It took all my strength not to fall apart, praying to mend the pieces of my broken heart. I spent so many nights feeling sorry for myself, oh how I cried and now I hold my head up high. Did you think I'd lay down and die?*
>
> *(Refrain) Oh no not I, I will survive as long as I have God to love I know that I'm alive. I've got all my life to live and all my love to give. I will survive. Hey, hey.*

My mind returned to the present when I heard one of my sisters in Christ recite instructions about dealing with our lifelong hurts and anguish. Some despairs, she told us, we were already aware of, while others were tucked away deep inside.

I felt better when she told us we would not be asked to share our memories with anyone else, nor did we have to write anything on paper.

I was reminded that God lives inside everyone and to prayerfully reflect on each of my hurts with an open heart. When ready to hand over each pain to the Lord, I was to release the thoughts at the foot of the cross. God waited to relieve me from my sorrows. As I relinquished each one, I'd feel the weight lifting off my shoulders. My heart would begin to heal, and peace and tranquility would enter my life.

There was no time limit. If I truly couldn't dismiss a pain after prayer, I was to move on to the next one. When I was finished with each of my despairs and had truly released my hurt at the base of the cross, God would take over my pains. For any unresolved hurts, I was to consider making an appointment with a priest or my counselor.

This felt right, and I was hopeful I would be able to hand all my pains over to the Lord.

Father Ronald said, "Let's slowly pray together the 'Our Father.' Please reflect on these words as you speak 'forgive us our trespasses as we forgive those who trespass against us.'"

As I spoke the 'Our Father,' the familiar tingling sensations came over me. I knew what God was asking of me, and I knew I needed help and growth if I were to forgive.

At the end of the prayer, the sanctuary of women sat in silence. I wasn't looking forward to bringing up old hurts. I wanted to hurry through my task, quickly forgive those I could, and hand my pains and sorrow over to God at the foot of the cross. I was well aware that I still had some unresolved pains. The question was, would I always have them, or would God, through some miracle I couldn't fathom, heal me?

My Lord God, I have no idea where I am going.
I do not see the road ahead of me.
I cannot know for certain where it will end. Nor do I really know myself,
and the fact that I think I am following your will doesn't
mean I am actually doing so.
But I believe that the desire to please you does in fact please you. And I hope
I have that desire in all that I am doing.
I hope that I will never do anything apart from that desire. And
I know that if I do this, you will lead me
by the right road though I may know nothing
about it. Therefore will I trust you always though
I may seem lost and in the shadow of death.
I will not fear, for you are ever with me,
and you will never leave me to face my perils alone.

CHAPTER THIRTEEN

Finding Forgiveness

Blessed Mary, Undoer of Knots,
pray for us through your grace, your intercession,
and your example. Deliver us from all evil and
untie the knots that prevent us from
being united with God, so that we, free from sin and
error, may find Him in all things. May
our hearts be placed in Him, and may we serve Him
always in our brothers and sisters. Amen.

—Pope Francis

Sitting in the hard pew, I shifted my weight, took a deep breath, and closed my eyes.

Unexpectedly, I shook with silent laughter. This task of resurrecting old hurts wasn't going to be difficult. I had no hurts to recall at birth or as a toddler, but as I continued to pray, the memory of the difficulty I'd had with the affirmation "I am beautiful" popped into my head.

As a tomboy growing up, I'd occasionally been called "fat" or "ugly." This teasing was meant to be harmless, but when repeated, I'd wondered if it might be true.

I thought of how, during my impressionable high school years, I was never picked to be on the homecoming court. This had bothered me then, but now it didn't matter in the least. It was my failed marriages that made me question whether I was truly beautiful and lovable.

Again, I silently asked myself, "Am I beautiful? Am I lovable?"

Truth be told, I still struggled sometimes to believe I was either. I needed to put this doubt at the base of the cross for once and for all, but I couldn't. Maybe my counselor Anne or my parish priest, Father David, could help.

Afraid of my next vision, I prayed and took a deeper breath. I felt tingling sensations as I thought about my younger brother. Silently, I asked God, "How can I ever forgive those involved with all of his pain? How can I forgive myself and release my guilt for not being able to save him? I want my brother back."

My body began to shake, and I sat in the pew crying as silently as I could.

Becca, the mother of a daughter I'd coached, noticed my distress and approached me with a box of Kleenex. She moved closer to me and rubbed my back. I turned and gave her a bear hug, weeping uncontrollably on her shoulder as the pain from James's death surfaced.

She whispered, "God and I are here for you. I will not leave your side until you want me to."

I tried to take deep breaths to control my tears. Silently, I prayed, "God help me. I don't think I can forgive. Please help me."

Unexpectedly, a poem by an unknown author called "I'm Free" entered my mind. I kept this poem inside my Bible, and it was as if I could hear my brother's voice reciting the words:

> *Don't grieve for me, for now I'm free. I'm following the path God laid for me. I took His hand when I heard Him call. I turned my back and left it all. I could not stay another day to love, to laugh, to work or play. Tasks left undone must stay that way. I found that place at the close of day. If my passing has left a void, then fill it with remembered joy. A friendship shared, a laugh, a kiss, ah yes, these things I too will miss. Be not burdened with times of sorrow. I wish you the sunshine of tomorrow. My life's been full; I savored much, good friends, well times, a loved one's touch. Perhaps my time seemed all too brief; don't lengthen it now with undue grief. Lift up your heart and share with me. God wanted me now. He set me free.*

I knew my guilt needed to be released to God, but I feared the base of the cross wasn't large enough to hold all my pain.

After praying the "Our Father," I gave my pain to God and handed over my guilt and forgiveness.

Tingling sensations rippled throughout my body, and I felt a sense of relief. I knew God and my brother were looking down on me with a smile.

I noticed some of the women were already leaving the sanctuary, but I hadn't released all my pain and sorrow yet. I recalled Father's instructions. Was I taking too long? Should I be finished already? I hesitated, then told myself, "No. I want my heart to heal."

I needed to forgive myself for being divorced. I had made the best choices I could at the time, but I wished I'd prayed harder to release the feelings of abandonment the dark side had placed upon my heart. I needed to ask my children for forgiveness so that I could forgive myself.

I then thought of an occasion after Wayne's death, at a time when public gossip and rumors were almost more than I could bear, when someone had taken a jab at me. Could I forgive her for laughing in front of a crowd and saying, "Hey Barb, whatever your last name is. You've had so many; I can't keep them all straight."

I'd stood silently, wanting to scream, and my friend had put her hand around my shoulder to comfort me.

Now I started to ponder which was better, to think something ugly behind someone's back or to say it to that person's face. My parents had always expressed that if you didn't have something nice to say, you shouldn't say it at all, but I too had occasionally uttered unkind words out of jealousy or in order to make myself look better.

Since Wayne's death, I'd spent significant time reestablishing my self-worth. Recognizing my flaws and my own humanity had helped me come to terms with some of those who'd hurt me. Nonetheless, I'd undergone so many painful experiences as a result of trusting others and conditional love. Was I capable of forgiveness? Would I ever be able to move forward?

Overwhelmed, I sat and sobbed. In spite of Father David's questions, and in spite of what I knew were the right answers, I could not honestly say my heart forgave those who had hurt me.

Becca sat comforting me, her hand around my shoulder, until I was ready to leave, even though I hadn't been able to release all my pain at the base of the cross.

I felt exhausted. Once again, it was all too clear that I had a lot of work ahead of me.

The next morning, while pouring a cup of coffee, a woman I had just met said, "You are so beautiful."

I looked over my shoulder and knew she couldn't be talking to me, but no one else was standing there.

When I faced her, a tear rolled down my face. Oh, how I wished I were beautiful.

Towards the end of Mass at the conclusion of the retreat, I began to thank God for all the witnesses I'd heard, and I also thanked Him for not asking me to be one. After Father Ronald blessed everyone with a beautiful prayer, the piano rang out as everyone sang, "Lead Me, Lord."

Although my own needs were still very apparent, I felt this retreat was the start of a changed life. I knew it had helped heal some of my brokenness and strengthened my relationship with God. My heart was on fire with the Holy Spirit, and I was inspired by the intertwined lives of all these Catholic women and their commitment to support one another and deepen their relationships with God. I wanted to build new friendships with these and other faith-filled women while continuing to work on forgiveness.

I began by looking in my Bible about the story of Joseph being sold, which I found in Genesis 37. His own brothers had betrayed him, yet he found goodness that came out of his situation along with love and forgiveness toward his family. Could goodness come out of my situation? Could I give up my anger and bitterness and hand control of my life to God?

Soon after the retreat, I called the rectory to make an appointment with Father David.

To my surprise, his secretary explained, "A parishioner hasn't shown up for his appointment. I will put you on hold to see if Father can see you right now."

She came back to the phone and asked, "Can you come in now?"

I hadn't expected this. I became anxious but answered, "Sure." I lived nearby, so I could get to the rectory quickly.

I tried to organize my thoughts. This must be what God had planned for me, so I drove straight to the rectory and waited in the reception area.

Father David greeted me with a big smile. In his gentle voice, he said, "Come into my office. Do you want some coffee or water?"

I quickly replied, "No, thank you. I must admit, Father, my thoughts are not organized, and I feel very unprepared for this meeting."

Father smiled. "Don't you worry. God has it all under control. Let's begin with a prayer and ask for God's intercession as you speak what's heavy on your mind."

After the beautiful prayer, Father assured me that whatever words were spoken in the room would stay between God and us.

I replied, "Father, you helped me through my trauma in the previous years, and I'm very thankful. I am here today to discuss forgiveness. At the retreat during reconciliation, you opened my heart to the possibility of forgiving. I truly want to heal and be able to forgive."

Father asked, "What is the source of your pain that doesn't allow you to forgive?"

I took a deep breath and said, "My marriages and being divorced. I can't forgive myself. I'm also still struggling with my miscarriage. Finally, I'm struggling to truly forgive all the people who were instrumental in the trauma I endured."

"Let's talk first about your miscarriage. Why can't you forgive yourself?" asked Father.

I explained, "I struggle to understand why I miscarried my baby. It must be something I did or didn't do right. They took him at the hospital, and I have no tombstone to visit. What am I supposed to do with all the empty feelings and pain?"

Father asked, "Do you believe your baby is with God?"

"Well, yes, of course he is with God," I slowly replied. The thought of God holding my baby immediately gave me comfort and joy.

"Your child who died before birth has gone before you in the presence of God. One moment in God's presence gives him more knowledge and love than we can gain in a lifetime. Your child knows you and loves you as his parents; he prays for you and watches over you. You should name him and count him as members in your family as you pray. Do you ever talk to your baby and ask for his help?" asked Father.

This question stunned me. I pondered it and answered, "I pray to God asking Him to take good care of my baby. I honestly never think to talk directly to my baby."

A tingling sensation came over my entire body, and my eyes started to well. From that moment on, I knew my baby was fine. I said, "Thank you, Father. Your insight is giving me comfort with a much clearer understanding."

I released another deep breath and said, "Two years after the miscarriage, I gave birth to our second child. Upon my return to work, feeling guilty about leaving my children at daycare, I was told I would be the switchboard operator instead of a secretary to a financial advisor. This is one of those events that I don't understand. What was God's plan for me?"

I told Father that with prayer and encouragement, I interviewed for a new job. God helped me land a secretarial job for a different financial institution, and I soon began a program to become a licensed financial advisor. Father nodded, and I continued.

"In the meantime, I was still feeling abandoned, and my marriage continued to struggle. Counseling did not help and nothing changed. I tried to concentrate my prayers to uncover a solution to give me some hope. I saw none and felt like a failure as our marriage ended in divorce. It makes me sad to think of how our children's lives have been impacted by our divorce. I wonder if they forgive me and if I will ever forgive myself."

Father asked, "Do you feel you did the best job you could as a mother?"

"I wish I'd known then what I know now, but at the time I did my best," I replied sorrowfully.

Father continued, "Did you ask for and receive forgiveness from God?"

I answered, "I repeatedly ask God for forgiveness. I understand that Jesus died on the cross to save me from my sins."

Father questioned whether I believed my words to be true. He said, "What right do you have to question His forgiveness by not forgiving yourself? If you are truly sorry and ask for forgiveness, then accept His gift. Forgive yourself and don't ask Him again."

I sat wide-eyed. I felt enlightened, but I needed time to ponder and accept God's gift. I excused myself and went to the bathroom to regroup myself.

"Do you truly love yourself?" Father asked me upon my return.

Embarrassed, I said, "Most of the time."

Father continued, "Why not all the time?"

"When God isn't the center in my life and I am not active in the church, or I make stupid decisions, I get down on myself and feel unfulfilled," I replied.

Father explained, "God dwells inside everyone. You must allow your heart to love yourself completely before you can love others completely. God will love you in good and bad times, but you need to also find a way to always love yourself. The Bible is one of the most inspirational and motivational books you can read. God is love. If you want to love yourself more, you have to get to know God more and love your creator more."

Tears rolled off my face, and I asked if I could have a drink of water.

Throughout my life, I'd made so many mistakes that brought pain to others and myself. Where was I to begin? I was far from perfect, and I knew I held onto and beat myself up for my decisions and actions. I'd sworn before God to stay married 'til death do us part' three times. Not keeping my promises hurt God, my spouses, my children, my parents, and of course myself. But even if I could forgive myself, how could I forgive Wayne and Deirdre?

Father came back into the room with a glass of water and asked me, "How does God's mercy of forgiveness make you feel?"

As I wiped my tears, I said, "I feel unworthy of his love. I want to forgive others and myself like God forgives me. I don't want his blood and sacrifice to go unnoticed in my life, but I don't know how to make my heart open up. I've placed a lot of layers around it to protect it."

Father asked me, "Right now, please pray as you bring up all the thoughts of unforgiving in your heart. Let me know when you are done thinking of all your bitterness."

I put my face into my hands with my elbows on my knees. I sobbed in silence for what seemed like forever. Finally, I lifted my head and wiped away my tears.

Father explained, "We are all human, and we all make mistakes. Freedom comes when you uncover all the bitterness and lack of forgiveness in your heart that steals life from you. Bitterness stems from pride and demands retribution. It's a proud guard around your heart. It demands answers and is fueled by your fears. It steals joy and peace from your life. Most people want to blame others. It makes you speak curses over others and usually you end up in bondage. Bitterness and lack of forgiveness have no place when God is sovereign over you."

He added, "Please sit quietly and think about what bitterness steals from you, what joy is taken from you. Can you find peace within? Does your soul feel free? When bitterness and lack of forgiveness take residence in your heart, how hard is it for you to love and trust?"

I felt overwhelmed. Father was absolutely correct. I had allowed joy to be taken from my life, and I still hadn't found complete peace. I definitely was fearful. Wanting a forgiving heart, I said, "Father, I want to put my pride aside along with my fears. How do I do this?"

Father replied, "God is enough, sufficient, and sovereign. When you stand secure in God's character, bitterness cannot keep you in bondage. Confront and replace your bitterness with God's truth. You will discover the freedom that comes with forgiveness. By truly believing in God, you are where you are supposed to be with a purpose that will stir up your spirit."

Father then said, "Right now, repeat the following to any bitter place in your soul: 'God is my refuge, my fortress, and my God whom I trust. I declare my faith in God who sees, knows, and promises to work all things together for me. Amen.'"

I repeated these words after Father, knowing this was a continuing challenge for me in my life of faith.

He then told me, "Remember Jesus's words on the cross: 'Father forgive them, they know not what they do.'"

I bowed my head. Simply saying these words was much easier than putting them into action, but I understood that I wasn't to despair while carrying my lingering pain and emotions. I also understood that Jesus, in His infinite wisdom, could see and say these words as part of His nature but that it was much harder for me as a mere human.

After I wrote these words down on a piece of paper, Father asked two things of me.

"Throughout each day, repeat the words, 'I completely love and accept myself the way God created me.' Also, I want you to daily recall all the good God has shown you and talk about it with me in our next appointment."

I began thinking about being the forgiver and also being forgiven. I needed to be honest with myself before I could ever really forgive because forgiveness included a degree of honest judgment of myself.

I left Father David's office renewed and ready to spread God's love, pondering the many blessings and miracles that had taken place in my life.

As time passed, I began to feel the sea change from "suffering servant and victim" to one rich in blessings and gratitude. I began to feel hopeful and joyful. The darkness was fading, and I felt peace in my heart that had never been there before.

For the first time, I realized I was beginning to forgive others and myself. I began thinking about how Wayne and Deidra, and others who had hurt me, were only human. I too was imperfect and had made poor decisions. Being human, I couldn't forgive everything immediately, but as I slowly opened my heart, I began to feel peace within.

Accordingly, with hope alive inside me, I joined about thirty other women and began preparations to host the next woman's retreat through Christ Renews His Parish. I began to read about how the Holy Spirit works, and finally I started to understand my tingling sensations.

Over the next six months, our group met weekly and grew to know one another at a deeper level. God unveiled to us how our lives intertwined, and I developed a very special bond with my sisters in Christ.

A couple of months before the retreat, we all gathered for discernment night. We had several topics to explore through a process encompassing prayer, Bible readings, and the guidance of the Holy Spirit. By the end of the night, our group would choose several witnesses to speak at the next retreat.

I felt uneasy as my sisters in Christ looked at me. I'd told them about the tingling sensations I often felt when God was nudging me, and they wanted to see if I was experiencing any now.

I was absolutely horrified when nearly all of the thirty-some women present chimed in together asking me to be a witness on scripture at the upcoming retreat.

I wanted to laugh and say, "Are you kidding? I have so much to read and comprehend. Scholars disagree on the meaning of the words, so what can I possibly say to help others?"

I couldn't help but recall the weekend of my first retreat. God must have laughed when I'd thanked Him for not asking me to be a witness. Though every ounce of my body screamed "Absolutely not," I prayed hard and the Holy Spirit again responded with tingling sensations.

I had to obey God. I would obey God. Slowly I answered, "Yes, I will be a witness."

Soon, the weekly meetings and countless hours spent preparing came to an end. As a group, with God's help, we were ready to put on the next women's Christ Renews His Parish retreat.

I would be speaking before a new group of over thirty women from the surrounding local parishes who were attending the retreat for the first time.

After the fact, I would find that this process of preparing to be a witness to scripture helped me uncover my new purpose in life—sharing my faith journey in order to help people heal, find hope and peace, know they're not alone, and glorify God.

Come, Holy Spirit. Replace the tension within me with a holy relaxation.
Replace the turbulence within me with a sacred calm.
Replace the anxiety within me with a quiet confidence.
Replace the fear within me with a strong faith.
Replace the bitterness within me with the sweetness of grace.
Replace the coldness within me with a loving warmth.
Replace the night within me with your day.
Replace the winter within me with your spring.
Straighten my crookedness. Fill my emptiness.
Dull the edge of my pride. Sharpen the edge of my humility.
Light the fires of my love. Quench the flames of my lust.
Let me see myself as you see me, that I may see you as you have promised me,
and be healed according to your word. Amen.

—Prayer to the Holy Spirit

CHAPTER FOURTEEN

WITNESS

May the strength of God guide me this day,
and may his power preserve me.
May the wisdom of God instruct me; the eye of God watch over me;
the ear of God hear me; the word of God give
sweetness to my speech;
the hand of God defend me; and may I follow the way of God.

The day of the retreat arrived. Most of my sisters in Christ were filled with excitement and nervous emotions while we engaged in last-minute preparations.

I prayed silently inside the chapel for an hour before giving my witness. I asked God for the courage to speak the truth of our relationship, and I prayed with all my might to speak His words, not mine.

When it was time, I walked slowly downstairs and into a room full of women. The music began to play the song I'd chosen, and it was "Beautiful" by Mercy Me.

God wanted me to do this, so I shouldn't have been surprised to feel tingling sensations as I walked towards the podium. I knew God's arms were wrapped around me.

When the music stopped, I was introduced as the next witness to talk on scripture. I grabbed a bottle of water, took a sip, and cleared my throat. I looked down at the papers on the podium, took a deep breath, and began to speak.

"God's words give me a new life filled with hope and choices that will allow love and peace to reenter my life. Today, I am going to share how God and scripture helped heal and save me."

The mood in the room felt welcoming as I explained my Catholic upbringing, my parents' devotion to one another and to God, and how I was taught the importance of God and family and given all the tools I needed to follow God. Then I confessed, "I still got lost along the way."

The thought of witnessing in front of women I did not know had filled me with fear, but my nervousness evaporated as I felt God's arms around me. Acknowledging my faults was easier than I had imagined it would be. God had given me the strength to work through and admit the spiritual paths I'd chosen.

Among other things, I explained my long inner struggle to understand the Bible. "When I first attempted to read the Bible," I admitted, "I tried to analyze the readings. I wished for more curiosity, a stronger faith, and a better understanding of what the Bible stood for: Basic Instructions Before Leaving Earth. I thought of the Bible as a book full of complicated names and stories too hard to read and understand. It wasn't until much later in life that I allowed God's words to speak to me. It's odd how the same readings at different times in my life have impacted me differently."

My audience looked sympathetic, and several women nodded as if they could relate.

I continued, "Two different sayings stay in my mind that are easier to recite than implement. The first one is this: 'In every situation, people either think negatively by looking at their cup as half empty or find the positives while seeing their cup as half full.' The other saying comes from God's words in Joshua 1:9, which says, 'Be strong and courageous; do not be frightened or dismayed, for the Lord your God is with you everywhere you go.'"

I knew God was with me, and I was grateful. I continued, "I want to tell you about my first miracle. It came when I was ten, when a tornado hit our family home."

I recounted the loud boom that had awakened me and my family's discussion on how God had saved us that night. I explained how, in the kitchen, one post remained standing with the phone still working—another gift from God. I recalled how my parents had counted our blessings.

I swallowed. "Now comes the hard part, talking about my failures. I am a sinner, and I am so thankful to God for dying on the cross for my sins. I have taken my gifts from God for granted. I have been a follower rather than a leader."

I explained the many mistakes I'd made growing up. I talked about my underage drinking and how I'd married right out of high school and divorced soon after completing my first two years of college. I confessed that I'd broken my parents' hearts, God's heart, and my own heart. I confessed that at that time, God was not the center of my life.

The room was silent, all eyes on me. I had to fight back my tears, but I still felt God's arms around me, which gave me the strength to continue to speak.

I explained how I completed my college education, lost part of my finger in a water skiing accident, and questioned whether it had happened as a consequence of being divorced, even though I knew God didn't work in this manner. I told how I began dating again and met someone special just before moving to Boston to start a new job. I explained how, within two years of meeting, we were married in the church and God became the center of my life once again.

I smiled. "All set to grow spiritually, I attended charismatic meetings and witnessed miracles and people talking in tongues. I began reading my Bible again. My goal was to read it from start to finish, but after a while, I became discouraged. The Bible is hard!"

I explained how my frustrations grew daily, how I more or less stopped reading God's word, and why my husband and I moved back home, where to my great joy, I realized God's plan was for me to become a mother, a job more important than anything I'd ever done before.

With the full attention of everyone in the room, I told about the birth of our first child, my joy in being a mother, my miscarriage, and the birth of my second child after another difficult pregnancy. I explained that deep down I wanted to stay home but that I needed to work full time to provide health insurance for our family.

I explained how difficult it was to work and care for the children while my husband worked out of town. I expressed my amazement that other mothers were able to do this. Finally, I revealed how my feelings of abandonment contributed to the end of our marriage, in spite of my attempts to seek counseling.

"The hole in my heart grew larger," I told the room. "I felt unlovable. Being divorced again made me feel ashamed. I had failed my children, God, my family, and myself. I wondered if my children would forgive me."

I explained how my children became my top priority. I talked about the two-year management program I was invited to participate in and the coaching I did for my kids' sports teams.

Then I told about meeting Wayne, my old boyfriend from junior high. I told how I started off not feeling like a good role model by marrying outside the church, how an accident served as a wake-up call, and how we later remarried in the Catholic Church.

I recounted James's death and how I would always remember the laughter and joy he brought to our family. I explained how I had to deal with my brother's death without my husband. I told about the hole in my heart over this as well as my guilt at not being able to save James. I conveyed my parents' heartbreak and pain and the depth of pain my brother must have endured.

I shared God's words from 1 Thessalonians 4:13–18 that helped comfort me then and still comfort me today: "Don't grieve as others do who have no hope. We believe Jesus died and rose again, even so, through Jesus, God will bring with him those who have died . . . Therefore encourage one another with these words."

I explained how, the following month, my husband and I discussed how I could retire as a financial advisor and work from home, allowing me more free time to be a mother and wife and also to do God's work with my mom, who led me to become a Eucharistic Minister at the hospital.

I explained that I felt unfit to do this ministry until 1 Corinthians 15:9–10 reminded me, "For I am the least of the apostles, unfit to be called an apostle . . . but by the grace of God I am what I am, and His grace toward me was not in vain."

I explained how this ministry filled me with joy and brought me even closer to God. I narrated the miracle healing that took place a year later allowing me to walk pain free, my surprise that my pain had been healed rather than my parents', and Father's reminder that "God's will be done, not my will."

I explained how my husband then accidentally skied into me, making it impossible for me to exercise. I confessed my struggle with this, asking, "How can a miracle healing be followed by anther injury?"

I conveyed how being overweight made me unhappy and shared John 6:63: "It is the spirit that gives life; the flesh is useless. The words that I have spoken to you are spirit and life."

To expand my faith, I explained how I attended parish classes on the topic of "finding your strengths." God had called me to serve, and I needed to know how. I admitted that even though I discovered my top five God-given strengths and was eager to serve, the devil constantly tested my faith.

Fighting back tears, I explained how, the next year, less than two months from my kids' graduations from high school and college, I had been betrayed by my husband and my girlfriend. I explained how, about nine months later, my former girlfriend's husband, who also was our family friend, killed my husband before killing himself.

From the looks on their faces, I could tell some already knew, but most of the women looked surprised and empathetic.

I chronicled the many deaths involved in this tragedy, including the death of our marriage vows, the death of my relationship with my husband's family, the actual death of my husband, the accompanying death of our friend, and the loss of feeling safe and secure.

I explained how my desire to be strong for my kids kept me going and how I kept repeating Isaiah 12:2: "God is my salvation. I will trust and not be afraid for the Lord God is my strength and my might."

I confessed how difficult it was to endure the drama and public gossip and how I prayed each night that my kids wouldn't be affected.

I told the crowd of women, "God gave me strength and courage every minute, every hour, every day, but broken, in shock, and embarrassed, I could only take one minute at a time."

Yet, I admitted, I knew others endured similar tragedies. I told how, throughout this traumatic period, God sustained me and Father David kept telling me how fortunate I was that God was bearing suffering upon me so that I would be prepared to do His works.

I looked out at the crowd of women. "One day, I finally understood what Father was saying after reading 2 Corinthians 12:10: 'Therefore

I am content with weaknesses, insults, hardships, persecutions, and calamities; for when I am weak, then I am strong.'"

I told how now, when people came up and asked how I'd survived, I answered, "God got me through each day."

I explained that when I prayed silently, I was able to hear and feel God's presence.

I explained that instead of praying to be rescued, I learned to ask to be redeemed.

Instead of praying for things to get easier, I learned to ask God to shape me in significant ways.

Instead of waiting for the scandal and trauma to be over, I learned something about patience.

"It was really hard to make peace with the uncertainty," I said, "but now I know that change is one of God's gifts to me. God is gracious and gives me new life. Healing comes through my tears. I believe my trials in this life are God's mercies in disguise."

I took a deep breath. Now was the hardest part of what God was asking me to do—to forgive others. I was to love my enemies and pray for those who persecuted me. I explained how, in spite of my efforts to forgive, my anger kept surfacing.

I recalled hearing a discussion on forgiveness and knowing that if I didn't forgive others, God would judge me in the same manner that I judged. I thought, "Who am I to cast judgment on others? Not forgiving is only hurting me."

I told the crowd of women that it wasn't until additional counseling with Father David and my personal counselor that I was able to leave my past hurts and struggles to forgive at the bottom of the cross. This wasn't an easy task, and it took a long time to complete, but finally I found peace in my heart.

"I am now able to say I forgive others *and* myself, and it was worth each and every painful step along the way. With God, anything truly is possible."

I also explained the tingling sensations I often experienced and how they made me feel unworthy and uncomfortable. I explained how often I ignored them until I finally asked Father, "What is God asking me to do?"

I smiled. "With Father's help, I realized that through these tingling sensations, God is allowing me to be in touch with the Holy Spirit. The Holy Spirit reminds me of God's love, goodness, and obligation to put God first in my life. 1 Timothy 4:13–14 says, 'Until I arrive, give attention to the public reading of scripture, to exhorting to teaching. Do not neglect the gift that is in you . . .'"

To this day, I confessed, I still didn't fully understand all that was written in the Bible, nor had I read God's word from cover to cover, though I'd become more familiar with many readings as I searched to find answers. I admitted that I often used my kids' *Catholic Youth Bible*, which offered simple indexes, searches, and readings that guided me to appropriate readings. At other times, I just opened up my Bible and began reading whatever page opened. Sometimes I found answers to other problems upon reading for several days.

I looked into the crowd, "Do I open up to these pages accidentally, or does God lead me to specific passages? I truly believe that God leads me."

I admitted, "I was broken, and God saved me. I now find God's words not just about death and rebirth but about life, hope, possibilities, and promises. God has awakened my curiosity so that I can grow spiritually. I can now say the scriptures move me and that I enjoy my new discoveries."

I added, "My pain and struggles caused changes in my life that were uninvited and undesirable, but it turned out that change was an opportunity for God's greatest gift of all to me. Over time, I was able to take my shattered pieces and make something beautiful and amazing out of my life. God gave me hope and helped me reclaim my life several times when I hit rock bottom. He made me the stronger, faith-filled woman I am today."

I then explained the importance of the God-loving friends who stood by my side throughout my trauma. I explained how God's work took place right in front of my own eyes when, at my first retreat, a wonderful woman with a smile and laughter that lit up the room said to me, "You are beautiful" and how much that meant to me at that particular moment.

I was almost finished, but I had one more thing to say. "Today when I hear the song 'Beautiful,' I actually *feel* lovable and beautiful. I am proud to be God's daughter, and my name is Barbara."

Women stood up and clapped. I had completed my task of being called to witness, and I believed my healing was complete. God had helped me reclaim my life after all my brokenness. No matter how many times I'd turned my back on God, He always opened his arms wide to receive me back into His life.

By now, I was fully aware that the depravity and suffering I'd experienced while trying to live apart from Him was not what I was put on Earth for. By contrast, God's unconditional love and forgiveness made me feel alive again.

As the song "Overcomer" by Mandisa began to play, a line formed to give me hugs of affirmation. I gladly opened my arms and took in each hug. God had been carrying me all along, and now He gently placed me on the ground. God knew I was ready to be obedient and start walking on my own towards Him.

Dear Lord Jesus, grant me divine intervention. Come into my life today.
Fill me with your Holy Spirit. Make me one with you. Walk with me today.
Dear Lord Jesus, give me the direction you wish me to go.
Fill my heart with the wisdom to know the path you set before me.
Dear Lord Jesus, fill my heart with your burning desire.
May your passion overtake complacency during my daily endeavors.
Dear Lord Jesus, give me the discipline to complete this journey.
When difficulty comes my way, give me strength, courage,
and knowledge to overcome.
In Jesus's name I pray. Amen.

—BY DOUG KUDWA

CHAPTER FIFTEEN

Girls Just Want to Have Fun

Thank you, Father, for having created us and given us to each other in the human family.
Thank you for being with us in all our joys and sorrows,
for your comfort in our sadness, your companionship
in our loneliness.
Thank you for yesterday, today, tomorrow,
and for the whole of our lives.
Thank you for friends, for health, and for grace.
May we live this and every day conscious
of all that has been given to us. Amen.

I don't believe that birth alone makes people sisters or brothers, though it makes them siblings and hopefully great friends some day, like my siblings and me. Growing up, I was taught that we are all brothers and sisters in God and that sisterhood and brotherhood are something we have to work at. Today, I believe that the quality of happiness between us grows in direct proportion to our acceptance of one another and in inverse proportion to our intolerance and expectations. True sisters and friends love and appreciate each other just the way they are.

As flawed as I might be, as out of place as I sometimes feel, and as lacking as I think I am, I don't have to hide all the imperfect pieces of myself from my sisters or girlfriends. They see my flaws as features that make me an interesting and beautiful daughter of Christ.

To the outside world, we may grow old, but we never grow old to our girlfriends, the extra sisters we choose for ourselves. My sisters and I know each other as we are. We know each other's hearts. We share private jokes. We remember feuds and secrets, grief and joys. We live outside the touch of time.

Sometimes when I least expect it, God places another sister in my life. For instance, my first retreat is not where I expected to make lifelong "sisters in girlfriends." I was still recovering from the horrific betrayal by my husband and girlfriend, but at all times, God knows my heart and what is best for me, and I am learning not to fight His will with my will, though this doesn't come easy.

Sisters understand the rules. They listen, do not try to fix or judge, and above all they pray for each other. I can reach for my phone at any hour of the day or night, and my girlfriends are right by my side. I can ask for their confidence, and they pray without any further questions. Of course, I do the same for them.

Sometimes, just thinking of all the memories I've made with my girlfriends makes me start laughing, and soon my cheeks hurt from laughing so hard. I've come a long way from being a tomboy playing sports with the boys to learning how special girlfriends can be. I feel blessed to be surrounded by so many loving girlfriends, and I'm grateful for the strength and courage God has given me so that I can trust again.

I want to make a difference in the world, so I try to reach out to those who seem to need help or to be alone. I do this very easily at church ministries and by helping out with missions for the homeless. I like to help people and make them smile. You never know when a gesture of kindness can make a difference in someone's life. I count my blessings each and every day for the individuals who stepped into my life when I was peeling myself off the floor.

I am still close to a few girlfriends from my twenties and many whom I met in the intervening years. I love them all dearly, but some of my fondest memories center around my sisters in Christ, my kettle bell friends, and a group of girlfriends from my hometown who gather or who already live near my oceanfront home. We walk on the beach and play golf or tennis, all while laughing and making new memories. No matter when or where I make friends, I hold them all close to my heart and in my prayers.

I know I have a true girlfriend when we don't speak in years and can immediately pick up where we left off without judging one another. I feel God put girlfriends on this Earth to give us another chance to show each other unconditional love.

I want to thank you, gracious God, for all the good friends you've given me;
They are a priceless gift. Thanks to you and their friendship, life is refreshing.
Due to your providence, God, I can count on the support
and help of my friends.
You have aided us in forming a solid bond
that can withstand all of life's threats.
The happiness you have blessed us with enables us to enrich one another.
Your loving power has given me this precious gift, and I am thankful.
I ask you, Gracious God, to keep them safe in your hands,
for they are yours above all. Amen.

*

CHAPTER SIXTEEN

Never Say Never

Love is patient; love is kind;
love is not envious or boastful or arrogant or rude.
Love does not insist on its own way;
love does not rejoice in wrongdoing, but rejoices in the truth.
Love bears all things, believes all things, hopes all things,
endures all things.
Love never ends. Amen.

—1 Corinthians 13

One day, comfortable with myself and continuing to grow in my relationship with God, I discovered a picture of a mother and her daughter accompanied by the verse quoted above from 1 Corinthians 13. The mother was asking her daughter to insert her boyfriend's name wherever the word "love" appeared as a way of deciding whether this boyfriend was the right one for her.

After Wayne's death, I began wearing a silver bracelet inscribed with this same verse. A close girlfriend gave it to me as encouragement to move forward.

True love does exist. I saw my parents love each other for sixty-eight years. I yearned for this same love, but I was afraid to try again, even though my counselor, Anne, encouraged me to open up.

I assured Anne that I was talking with my dad, brothers, and uncles, but there was no way I was going to the bars to meet men. Besides, I had my girlfriends and family for companionship.

Anne laughed and said, "Going to the bars isn't exactly what I'm talking about. How about after church you ask a single man out to coffee? Come back to see me when you are ready and tell me how you would like to meet someone."

The challenge was on, as I was going to attempt meeting a man in my own way and on my own terms. After some time, I discovered my way wasn't working and that I needed God's help.

Shortly thereafter, I set up an appointment with Father David to talk about my trust issues. We started with a prayer and then discussed all my relationships and what I thought went wrong with each one.

During our discussion, the light went on. Each of my challenging relationships had in common the simple fact that God wasn't the center of my life. I was always looking for something that was right in front of me.

Father told me to stop trying to search for earthly love before I truly felt and understood God's agape love. It was there for my taking, he assured me. Every minute of every day, I could receive unlimited, selfless, sacrificial, unconditional love from God. He was the true lover of my soul, my bridegroom, and my Savior.

Why did it take me so long to accept that God is my bridegroom? That He is everything I need? Why did I fall away from Him time after time after time?

I knew the answer. I wanted to control my own life. I also knew I had to give up all my control and give it to God. Handing all my control over to God wasn't going to be an easy task. Likewise, meeting a faith-filled man was going to be easier said than done!

After a couple of months, I began talking with a Catholic man from a big Catholic family. Needless to say, I had many questions. How was I to know if God was leading us together? Was God front and center in his life? Did he follow God's will and not his own? Would our friendship allow us to pray and grow together spiritually?

I soon learned that we had a lot in common. Both of us believed in God and praised Him at weekly mass, and we also both had a younger sibling who'd passed away. We both had two loving adult children, we had both coached sports, and we both enjoyed playing golf and tennis. In addition, we both wanted to travel during retirement.

Slowly, over time, I learned to trust him and began to confide in him. For months, we talked on the phone for hours at a time and regularly emailed each other. He made me smile and laugh.

After several months, we finally met for a date. Happily, the final piece was there. We were instantly attracted to one another, but he lived several hours away, which made dating a little difficult.

I lived in the town where my parents and siblings lived, while he lived far away from his hometown and his siblings. Family was a very important part of my life, and he understood that I wanted to be close to my aging parents. Sadly, both his parents had passed before we met. He met my golfing friends who had given me the support and encouragement I needed to get me through the toughest of times, and I met his friends who had helped support him. I was retired and he was partially retired, so we saw each other as often as we could.

After dating for almost two years, we became engaged at a restaurant after celebrating with his adult children. I prayed that he would desire to do God's will, that he would lead and speak words that built me up and built our family up while reflecting God's love. I prayed he would submit his schedule to the Lord and find joy and peace with his relationship with God, pursuing only those goals that bring God glory and that count for eternity. I prayed that our marriage would be blessed and flourish with only love and forgiveness until the end of our days.

When we met with our parish priest, he shook my fiancé's hand and said, "She's been through a lot. You'd better be good to her."

Because I still questioned my decisions, we then met with Anne, my counselor. Having had the floor pulled out from beneath me before, I wanted to make sure my wonderful new fiancé understood my trauma, how my parents had always been my rock, and how important family was in my life.

We also traveled many miles by car to see several of his and my family members. It was fun to hear stories about him, to see the area he grew up in, and to listen as his family teased him that he was the lucky one in this relationship.

To reassure me, my fiancé listed examples of when he'd persisted in the face of problems in past relationships and how he kept his word, and I saw him happily attend weekly mass to give thanks and praise. We agreed to work through any problems, both of us ready to move forward in marriage with God.

We took pre-marriage classes taught through our parish and each chose a mentor we could talk with on a daily basis. We knew life would bring change, and we each chose a mentor we felt comfortable with. During stressful times, we committed to immediately contact our priest, mentor, or counselor.

We happily married with all four of our adult children by our sides, joining as one big happy family with God at the center of my life. We both understood that marriage was hard work and that we would have to learn how to combine our new lives into one. Later we did experience difficulty in combining our new lives together, but the main thing we had in our favor was God. Through trial and error, we needed to discover how to combine our lives into one that God approved of while keeping Him front and center.

For example, shortly after our marriage, I stepped on top of a tennis ball, rolled my foot, and broke the outer bone. Three months later, with no healing taking place, the doctors discovered I had nerve damage. I began to take nerve medication, all the while praying this problem would be temporary.

Thus our first issue to work through—taking care of one another in sickness and in health—came early in our marriage. Since I was younger than he was, I'd assumed I'd have to take care of him first, not the other way around. Even though he became ill the following year and I took care of him for several months, neither of us was comfortable depending on someone else, but we made the best of it.

Meanwhile, he was a trooper, helping me until I could help myself. I tried to stay positive while praying for healing, and I learned to become creative in moving around with my knee scooter.

Nine months passed, and I was still praying for my foot to heal and to be able to exercise or even just walk again without pain. Then one of my retreat sisters asked if I was open to alternative healing and gave me the name of a healer, Linda Franklin, specializing in foot zone therapy, craniosacral therapy, and esoteric healing.

I was open to anything at this point, but I was thrilled to discover that Linda believed in God. I felt God was using her as a vessel to help make a difference in people's lives.

I went to her home and immediately sensed warmth, love, and security. I felt safe and began to feel tingling sensations throughout my body. Amazingly, at my first session, Linda assisted in the healing of my foot, and I shouted to heaven with joy and gratitude. The Divine Healer relies on the competency of earthly helpers, and I thanked Him for inspiring and giving her the gift to heal me.

I was experiencing God's full circle of unconditional love, and to this day, my foot continues to be healed.

God is good all the time!

Lord, no eye has seen, no ear has heard,
no heart has conceived the things
you have prepared for those who love you.
Set us ablaze with the fire of the Holy Spirit,
that we may love you in and above all things
and receive the rewards you have promised us
through Christ our Lord. Amen.

CHAPTER SEVENTEEN

Celebration of Life

God of power and mercy, you have made death itself
the gateway to eternal life.
Look with love on our dying brothers and sisters, and make them
one with your Son in his suffering and death,
that sealed with the blood of Christ,
they may come before you free from sin.
We ask this in your name. Amen.

One year after our marriage and four years after Wayne's death, my husband returned home from spring break to coach, while I stayed put at our ocean home to tackle the yearly house cleaning.

Shortly thereafter, I received a call telling me my dad had fallen. There were no broken bones, but his recovery would take place in rehab at the hospital.

My dad was ninety years old and going strong, so there was no reason to rush home, but no one could have guessed how the following month would play out.

Soon I received another call, this one from my dad. He wasn't doing well, and I needed to get home as quickly as I could. I knew it was possible that these were his precious final words.

Waiting for my connecting flight after completing the first leg of my journey, I overheard the couple next to me say, "Why don't they know if we'll get home by tonight?"

I jumped out of my chair and ran to the check-in desk. "I don't see any delays on your screen. Is it true I may not make it home today?"

"Yes, ma'am," came the confirmation. "I'm really sorry, but with all the delays and storms from yesterday, all our flights are off schedule and overbooked."

My breathing came fast. I cried out, "This can't be happening! My father is dying, and I need to get home right now!"

"Please take it easy, Ma'am. Let me see your ticket, and I'll call the manager and see what he can do. In the meantime, have a seat and I'll be right back with you."

I quickly replied, "No, thank you. I'll wait right here."

I began to pray for God's help. After a half hour that seemed like eternity, I was placed on a waiting list with ten other people. This was the best they could do.

Wiping my tears, I ran to the next hub and stood there praying. My tears would not stop. A lady with a baby gave me some tissues and asked, "Are you all right?"

Sobbing, I explained, "I'm on a wait list. My father is dying, and I must get home to see him today."

God answered my prayers when the woman reached into her purse and handed me her ticket, saying, "Let's go up to the counter to let them know you can use my ticket."

I stood there in shock. Finally, I said, "Thank you, but you have a child. Don't you need to get home today too?"

She replied, "God led me to you. I'm going to be fine. Please, use my ticket."

As was so often the case, God sent me an angel and answered my prayers. I gave the woman a great big hug as my tears fell.

I returned too late to hear my dad speak again, but he was still alive, and I was going to hold tightly to the words we'd shared over the phone. I never would have guessed that God had another miracle in store for us.

It was my dad's final week on Earth, and our family surrounded his bed. It was a Friday in April, but just not any Friday. Today was my parents' sixty-eighth wedding anniversary.

My dad could not speak, but we were assured he could hear every word we spoke. The hospice nurses encouraged us to keep talking, and my mom suggested we celebrate with a cake. The nurses opened up the cafeteria and wheeled in my dad in his bed.

Mom sat down in a chair next to him and started reading him their anniversary cards. I couldn't believe the strength and courage she possessed. When she finished the last card, with so much tenderness and affection, she told him, "I love you" and leaned over for a kiss.

We were all shocked when my dad moved his lips to kiss her back. I thought this was the best anniversary gift she could ever have received. A true miracle had occurred.

Two days later, my father faded away. His golden heart stopped beating, and his hard-working hands were crossed and laid to rest.

I stayed by his side until the funeral home took him away.

The next three days were a blur of preparations for the visitation and funeral, but I hold tightly to the vivid memory of my mom walking behind my dad's casket at the end of the funeral singing "Jerusalem, My Destiny" with her whole heart and soul while looking up to Our Lord.

The following day, shaken from the conflicting emotions of grief and joy, I flew with my husband to celebrate my grown child's wedding. Surrounded by the love of family and friends, I saw an absolutely stunning bride and a handsome groom. The wedding was memorable, elegant, and picturesque. I was very proud and happy for them, and I felt blessed to have another family member.

Unbelievably, another miracle soon occurred. Forty days passed, and my dad's birthday came. My mom was filled with grief, and in my prayers that night, I cried and asked God to take away her pain.

The next morning, I awoke with a small feather on top of my Bible. I wondered where it had come from, since I don't have a down comforter or pillows. After thinking about it, I concluded this was an angel's feather, a sign that God was going to take care of my mom's grief.

Little did I know how he intended to care for her. Two days later, early on a Monday morning, having barely begun to grieve my father's death, my mom's heart stopped beating and she unexpectedly passed away.

How could this be? She was so full of life! We had watched the sun set together just the previous evening! We had planned to attend Mass together this morning!

I was plagued with questions. How could my father's fall have caused his death? Had my mother actually died of a broken heart? How could I cope without them?

Within four days, my mother's visitation and funeral had taken place. My husband asked if it was all right if he coached his team at the high school state finals the same day as my mom's funeral. I said yes and made arrangements with the funeral home so we could visit my mother together before he left town.

My children and family all supported me as unbearable grief from the death of both my parents struck me hard during the funeral.

Sitting on their dock after my mom's service, I was unable to move. I actually felt paralyzed, with so much pain in my chest that I could barely breathe. How was I to find meaning and purpose without them?

I was almost sixty years old, but I felt abandoned, orphaned, and alone. Could you be an orphan at my age? I knew that God my Father was with me wherever I went, but still I felt parentless. My parents had stood by my side through every event of my life, the good as well as the horrific. I had talked to them on the phone often and made sure I saw them frequently. They had taught me about God and how to pray. They had shown me by example how to love unconditionally. The one thing they hadn't taught me was how to live without them.

Each night, I continued to visit my parent's home, sitting with my legs crossed on the edge of their dock. Each night, I continued to find myself in a trance. Sometimes I heard music in my head. My parents had loved the song "Amazing Grace," and we had played it at both their funerals.

In desperation, I began seeing a bereavement counselor who told me my grief was natural, but I found nothing natural about it. I was told the length of my mourning would be linked to the depth of the relationships I mourned. I asked God, "Will I ever stop mourning?"

One Sunday after Mass, I told Father David, "I don't want to accept that my parents are gone."

He replied, "I miss your father and mother too, but it's God will, not your will, be done. Your parents obeyed God. Be happy and proud of them. They are together for eternity, jubilant and waiting for you to join them someday. On Earth they were limited, but now it's endless what they can do for you. Know they are still with you and watching over you every day."

I awakened each morning with my Bible and a pile of sympathy cards on my bed stand. Each morning, unsure of how many tears were left, I read one more sympathy card. Inside one special card was a piece of paper titled "Holy Trinity" that read:

> *O God, Thou who art one in nature and three in persons, Father, Son, and Holy spirit, first cause and last end of all creatures, the infinite Good, incomprehensible and ineffable, my Creator, my Redeemer, and my Sanctifier, I believe in Thee, I hope in Thee, and I love Thee with all my heart.*
>
> *In the midst of Thine infinite happiness, Thou didst choose me, through no merits of mine, in preference to countless other creatures who would doubtless have corresponded with Thy blessings better than I have done; Thou didst love me from eternity; and when my hour in time had come, Thou didst draw me from nothingness into earthly existence and didst bestow upon me Thy grace, as a pledge of everlasting life.*
>
> *From the depths of my misery, I adore Thee and I give Thee thanks. Thy holy Name was invoked over my cradle to be my profession of faith, my plan of action, and the only goal of my earthly pilgrimage; grant, O most Holy Trinity, that I may ever be inspired by this faith, and may carry out this plan with perseverance, so that, when I have reached the end of my journey upon earth, I may be able to fix my gaze upon the blessed splendors of Thy glory. Amen.*

I clung to this prayer through each blurry day and long sleepless night. I moved as if in a fog, but a smell, sound, or memory could turn on the faucet of tears at any moment. Out of habit, I would pick up my cell phone to call my parents only to throw it down in disbelief, tears raining down my face.

I would have given anything to see them or hear them speak one more time. It helped to know they were in a much better place and no longer felt any pain.

My counselor reminded me that everyone grieves differently and that grieving is necessary for healing. She also reminded me that there is no time limit to the grieving process and told me not to feel pressured by those who didn't understand my needs, pain, and emptiness.

I was blessed with support and comfort from my family, friends, pastor, and congregation, and I clung tightly to God, my prayers, and the Bible.

Could I heal from this loss? I wasn't sure, but time would tell. All I knew was that life as I'd known it would never be the same. It felt like memories were all I had left to cling to, but because my parents were with God, I turned anew to the creator and my redeemer.

O my Lord God, here I am! You created me and know me completely.
You know all about my life, my joys and my suffering,
my questions and my dreams.
I know you love me, even when I feel my sins and
mistakes make me unlovable.
Help me to love you, God, with all my heart, mind, and soul,
and to love all the people even as I love myself.
Jesus, thank you for showing me how to live.
I know you want only the best for my life, and
I believe that following you is the way to a full and abundant life.
Holy Spirit, give me the courage and wisdom
to be Jesus' follower, even when it isn't easy.
Fill me with the joy and peace that comes from doing your will. Amen.

*

CHAPTER EIGHTEEN

Who Am I?

O my God, I came unto the earth naked and penniless and
I will leave the earth the same way,
with you only as my eternal goal.
Let me know myself: let me know thee,
and desire nothing else but thee.
Let me love myself only if I love thee,
and do all things for thy sake.
Let me humble myself and exalt thee,
and think of nothing else but thee.
Look upon me that I may love thee,
call me that I may see thee, and
forever possess thee, for all eternity
through Jesus Christ, our Lord. Amen.

Just over seven months after my parents passed, I lost my best friend, the one who had stood by my side through thick and thin. He always made me smile, and he was a fantastic listener who never tried to fix, keep tabs, or judge, always comforting me and licking my tears away.

Putting Duke down was one of the hardest decisions I've ever had to make. My heart ached, and I missed him fiercely. He'd been part of my daily life for fourteen years, and without him, I felt even more lost. Not surprisingly, I pushed the pain downward, as I was still trying to grasp my parents not being on Earth to love, hold, and laugh with.

My parents, my foundation and solid rocks throughout my life, no longer lived on Earth, and I needed to process the significant impact of losing them. Even though my faith was intact, I sought help from an organization that works with those who are grieving the death of a loved one.

One day at the grief center, a very beautiful, loving, and spiritual woman enlightened me as to why my world felt so broken. She told me that grief and trauma affect everyone differently and that grief is something personal that lives forever. She also told me that with healthy healing and support, it didn't need to define me. If I were to survive, I needed to discover what my new normal was by processing each individual loss that had entered my life. Not working through each loss or tragedy allowed the one that followed to add to the initial pain and suffering and become indistinguishable from the first.

It took me time to understand that I would not be able to heal from today's grief without working through these prior events.

My counselor shared many things with me, including some that I already knew but simply needed to develop a deeper understanding of. Although I felt God's presence and His power, my heart bled and my body ached with emptiness.

I told my new counselor that when James died, my foundation was shattered and I was filled with more emotions than I knew what to do with. My expectations for the natural order of life, with my parents growing old together and dying before any of their children, had been destroyed. I admitted that I'd found it much easier to push the pain aside than to deal with it. I later learned this was one reason I couldn't answer the question, "Who am I?"

My counselor explained to me that as the daughter of grieving parents, my life had changed dramatically. I had to process James's absence in my life, in our lives, and figure out how to continue without him. Essentially, my role changed from daughter and sister to grieving daughter and grieving sister. Life would never be the same, and I needed to find a way to embrace my new role.

She also explained how my role changed with each divorce. Going from wife to ex-wife meant losing my identity, my marriage, my best friend and defender, my husband, my husband's family, and also some friends. With each loss, I needed to rediscover who I was.

I also came to understand that I was grieving not only the loss of each individual, whether through death or divorce, but also the loss of my expectations. I was lost and broken because these, too, had been destroyed. Now I needed to start over and uncover what my new normal would be while developing new expectations. This meant discovering who I was in each new role after each loss.

My counselor talked about the importance of mourning each loss, allowing the pain in, learning tools to work through the pain, and finding a support system of people who cared. This was especially important now that I no longer lived full time in my hometown with my family and parents by my side. After my marriage, I had even taken a leave of absence from the country club, and a full two years passed without me seeing all my friends and support group.

With my counselor's help, I began praying, counseling, and unveiling what my new support group might look like while learning coping skills and identifying and working on new goals.

I needed to do all these things for each loss I'd experienced in order to find healthy healing, but it wasn't easy. It required understanding, love, patience, and time. Happily, I discovered there is hope beyond belief and that I am not alone in my grief and sorrow. I found others who didn't judge me but who instead gladly supported me and shared my grief journey.

Grabbing God's hand with hope, I began working on rebuilding my foundation, finding my new normal, and discovering who I am. I started with the loss of my unborn child and am working on each subsequent loss in my life over several decades.

I discovered that I am human and that I make mistakes. A friend of mine suggested that they are not so much mistakes but rather opportunities for God to help me grow. Today, I like to think that with each difficulty I've had, I've been able to learn something significant about myself, about how to live despite loss and pain, and how to find hope in healing.

I also finally learned once and for all that it's important to forgive others, no matter how difficult, in order to release the anger and bitterness and to find peace and happiness. I also learned the importance and necessity of asking for forgiveness and forgiving myself. Seeking forgiveness first from others was both challenging and courageous. After all these years, I admit that forgiving myself was not only my most difficult task I faced but also the most necessary.

I am not just a bystander of Christ's suffering on the cross. I am not just watching and wondering what it would be like to be raised by the glory of the Father and join Him someday in eternal life. Today, I am taking an active role to follow Him.

I am a child of God who has suffered intense pain and received hope anew through His unfailing, unchanging, and unconditional love, grace, and mercy. Finding God anew saved me and gave me my life back, the life with His daily presence that I no longer take for granted.

Despite all my tragedy and trauma, today I know that God was always present in my life. Each time I was broken, God peeled me off the floor and built me into His stronger disciple. Even when I did not feel worthy, God never gave up on me and always stood beside me or carried me when I didn't have the strength to walk. He was with me even when my prayer life suffered and I felt like I didn't deserve His love.

Who am I? I am a child of God who is loved by Him no matter what. My other roles in life may change, but through the love that can only come from Him, my role as a daughter of our Lord will never change. This I know for certain.

O God, with whom there is no darkness, but the night shines as the day:
keep and defend us and all your children, we beseech you,
throughout the coming night.
Renew our hearts with your forgiveness,
and our bodies with untroubled sleep,
that we may wake to use more faithfully your gift of life,
through Jesus Christ, our Lord. Amen.

EPILOGUE

Good Morning, God

Good morning God, our Father, we thank you for
waking us to see the light of this new day.
Grant that we may waste none of its hours,
soil none of its moments,
neglect none of its opportunities, fail in none of its duties.
And bring us to the evening time undefeated by any temptation,
at peace with ourselves, and with you.
This we ask for your love's sake. Amen.

Six months after my parents died, I found blessed peace at an All Souls and All Saints Mass where I was asked to remember all our saints who endured suffering and to pray that all souls be saved from the fires of hell, especially those most in need of God's mercy.

I said these prayers for all those who had passed away. I prayed for my parents, thought about them, talked with them, and asked for their help.

With all my heart, I believed my parents were with God. My spirit was also with God. Therefore, we were together, always and forever.

Nonetheless, the "firsts" brought heartache. The first time walking into our home without my parent's to greet me. The first Thanksgiving dinner without Dad leading the prayer and hearing what he and Mom were thankful for. The first time I took pictures of them for their following year Christmas cards, but was unable to send them out. The first Christmas that I didn't help them decorate or celebrate in our family home. This year, I will soon encounter their first birthdays and their first wedding anniversary without them present to experience and create new memories.

In the meantime, I will try to fill the void with love and laughter from family and friends. My husband will soon be retired, and we will embark on our future together. Joyous celebrations lie ahead. My youngest will be married soon, blessing us with another family member, and other family members blessing us with two more grandbabies. I absolutely love our grandkids and being a grandma! They fill my heart with such pleasure and restore my zest for life and faith in humanity.

As time passes, I continue to find hope, healing, and renewal. I am able to share my fond memories, and as family members share their stories, I start to understand why the words "celebration of life" are so often used at funeral services. From my parents, I learned that at the end of each day, I should answer the question, "Were my actions today rewarding to God or regretful to God?"

My goal each day is to make my actions rewarding to God, who died on the cross and gave me new life. My sins are forgiven and His death shall not be in vain. Life on Earth is but a blink compared to eternity, and when I die, I will have to answer to God.

I don't fear death any longer because I now understand the bigger picture. My faith helps me to uncover my purpose here on Earth and reminds me that there is everlasting life with God.

Amen!

Lord, help me to accept that everything is done in your time, not mine.
I am so thankful for all the love and joy my parents brought into my life.
Please help my family and me heal emotionally, physically,
and spiritually from all our grief.
Please help my family memories that bring tears and sorrow
turn into comfort and peace deep within all our hearts
for the rest of our days.
Help us to be able to celebrate our parents' lives both here on Earth and
with you, Christ our Lord, in Heaven. Amen.

*

About the Author

Barbara Kudwa worked as a financial advisor with an emphasis in presenting seminars. Over time, she found God calling her to witness to His unconditional love, grace, and mercy. Using her spiritual journey filled with challenges and healings, she now seeks to inspire others to allow God to impact their lives. Acting as a catalyst for hope in the midst of darkness, she reveals in *Finding God Anew* how she experienced miracles, counseling, a reviving retreat, and forgiveness. She also speaks on these topics at religious conferences, retreats, and at not-for-profit organizations. For more information, visit www.barbfindsgodanew.com.